BET YO[ ]
DIDN'T
KNOW
IT COULD
DO THAT

Life Hacks that'll Blow Your Mind

- Accomplishing More by Doing Less
- Hacking the Hell Out of Life
- Life simplified

RAFAEL GURKOVSKY

Want to read more exciting stories for **FREE?**

Join my V.I.P List now!

I regularly GIVEAWAY FREE books and SPECIAL DISCOUNTS!

Join my mailing list and be one of thousands we already receiving FREEBIES!

Join by visiting this site:

http://www.ravenspress.com/freeselfhelp/

Or Scan this QR Code from your smartphone to go the website directly

RAVENS PRESS

ISBN-13: 978-1519153562

ISBN-10: 1519153562

http://www.ravenspress.com/freeselfhelp/

TABLE OF CONTENTS

INTRODUCTION

The term 'hack' was widely used to refer to someone gaining unauthorized access to another person's computer, email, or some other online account. Later on, the world was also applied to software and games. For instance, if a game has certain rules and limitations coded into it, certain things that you are not allowed to do or need a certain level of in-game experience to do, you could hack it and make them go away. Hacks were, and still are, used to modify all those things to make the games easier to play, to bend the rules to our will, and take the whole gaming experience to another level. But the hacks I am going to tell you about in this book, the life hacks, are going to change your life.

In life, there are common problems that we find hard to solve but in reality you can find solutions to these common problems with the help of some tricks, tips and hacks. Some solutions are so simple and readily available.

In the modern world, technology has played a great impact in your daily life. Most of the activities you do involve something about technology. Here are some of the technology hacks that can help you.

1. Using Lego Figurines to Hold Your Cords

2. Using a Drawer to Keep Your Electronics Organized

3. Cleaning You Keyboard with a Swipe
Use the sticky ends of a Post-it to clean in between your keyboard keys.

4. Bumping Music Out of a Cup

You can place your smartphone in a glass, paper or plastic cup to amplify the music. It's your own DIY speakers.

5. Protecting your Charger Cord

Get a pen spring and wrap it on the cord of your charger. This protects your cord from bending and breaking.

6. Organizing your Cables and Cords

You can make use of bulldog clips to hold your cables. Just place them at the back or side of your desk.

7. Avoid Sending Out Incomplete Emails

When composing an email, leave the recipient field blank. Enter the email address when you are done composing your email.

8. Making your Own Earphone Holder

Avoid having tangled earphones by securing the cords on a wooden spool.

9. Using a Shoe Box to Keep your Cords and Rolls of Toilet Paper to Keep them from being Tangled.

10. Using Old/Used Cassette Cases as a Phone Holder or Stand.

11. Using Accented Letters to Make Your Passcodes More Secure.

12. Using Binder Clips to Repair your Keyboard's Broken Feet/Stand.

13. Using Bread Clips in labelling and organizing your chargers, cables and power cords.

14. Increasing Battery of your Android

You can use two methods in order to increase the battery of life of your android gadget.

a. Adjust your animation scales in the Settings of your device. Go to "About Phone," tap the "build" option 7-10 times. Go back to the Settings and choose Developer Option. Set the Window Animation Scale, Animation Duration and Transition Animation Scale to 0.5 or you can opt to turn them off.

b. Use the Greenify app, make sure your device is rooted before using this app. You need to download and then install the Greenify App. Open the application and allow its superuser access. Tick on the + button and click on Tick.

15. Finding your Lost Android Phone

Go to Security Settings, then Device Administrator and then activate it. Go to Google Play Store and click the Gear Icon on. Choose the Android Device Manager, after the system finds your device you can see three options: Ring, Lock and Erase. Choose the option that you prefer.

These are only a few of the many technology hacks you can do that can help you make your daily routines and activities easier and better.

In your everyday life, it is very likely that you will encounter troubles that will make things inconvenient for you. Wherever you may be, life will probably come up with a way to make things stressful. Your stress can come from many different sources. From something as simple as getting an odor out of your clothes to something as important as being more productive at work.

Do not allow these tiny inconveniences to ruin your day! You can easily solve problems and issues by learning life hacks! Life hacks will give you the power to deal with stress and small problems in a very graceful way. It will make your life easier and much more convenient.

LIFE HACKS TO INCREASE YOUR PRODUCTIVITY

Ever wake up thinking today will be the day you'd get a lot of work done, and then at the end of the day you realize you've "successfully" watched through all first 3 seasons of House of Cards? If your productivity level only extends to making coffee in the morning, then it's time to kick it up a notch! Following are some life hacks that can make you do more and end the day with a smug "I'm the man" look on your face...

2 Minutes

The two minute rule simply states that if you are confronted with a task that takes only two minutes to finish, then do it right now and get it over with! Don't leave it hanging because pretty soon, you'll have a collection of 2-minute tasks that would take an hour to complete. Just finished your mug of coffee? Wash it immediately within 1 minute and you'll never have to face a dirty sink again.

Create a priority list

Lists are a great way to get organized and the more organized you are, the more productive you'll be. However, rather than just jotting down the things you need to get done, list your tasks by how important they are (with the most important task being at the top). You'll realize that once you've gotten through the hard stuff, the simple ones will be much easier for you to check off the list.

Time your tasks

Yes, at times you'll have the most tedious things to take care of and you'll sit for hours procrastinating because you're reluctant to star, dreading how long it will take until you're through. The more you procrastinate, however, the less you get done. If the length of the task is what bothers you the most, allocate a certain amount of minutes (say 5) and when this time is up, move on to something else for another 5 minutes and then back to the 'tedious' task. In doing so, you won't have to sit through the same thing for long stretches of time, but you'll still be able to get it done.

Seinfeld Calls It!

Jerry Seinfeld is magic when it comes to stand up! But how exactly did he achieve such a high level of expertise? Practice, of course! He made sure that a few hours each day are dedicated to stand up practices. To boost his motivation, Seinfeld started putting an X mark on the calendar for every day he practiced. The satisfaction of seeing an unbroken line of X's motivated him into NOT breaking the chain. Try it!

Procrastinate Productively

Now this sound like an oxymoron, but it actually makes sense. Notice how you are trying to distract yourself with practically anything just to avoid doing work that you hate? Instead of walking around burning precious time, you can try doing something else that you don't "hate" as much. For example, procrastinate while cleaning up your inbox or perhaps start straightening out your desk to make it more work friendly. There are lots of productive procrastination steps that you can do, and each one would help you shift your focus from the task you don't want to do with the task you can tolerate to do until you're ready for the real thing.

Make a Playlist

Have you seen Inception where Leonardo DiCaprio uses a song to time his way into a dream? When it reaches the chorus, he knows it's almost time to wake up from the dream. You can do this too (while awake, of course) by creating a playlist that tells you whether you're on time or not. Try putting together a 30-minute playlist and start playing it the minute you wake up. The goal is to make sure that before the last song in the playlist ends, you're already in your car and driving to work. You can also link the songs to the activity you're supposed to be doing (breakfast while listening to Neil Young, The Black Keys while taking a bath, etc.), allowing you to easily judge whether you're slacking or not.

Know your Optimum Productivity Hour

Every person has that time of the day where they're positively brimming with energy. For most, it's in the morning right after a dose of coffee while others are at their best after-lunch. No matter what your optimum time happens to be, identify it and make the most of it during your working hours.

Get the Temperature Right

Studies reveal that the right temperature can actually increase or decrease your productivity. According to Cornell research, the magic number is 77 degrees Fahrenheit, allowing you to be perfectly comfortable and focused on the job. You might want to let your boss know about this number and if the office isn't just willing to pay the bill, you can also try to affect the temperature yourself. Bring a portable fan or layer your clothing, depending on the circumstances.

Make Your Breakfast Exciting

What can motivate you to wake up early? Excellent breakfast, of course! Just the thought of freshly made coffee can get you up and about within minutes. To make this happen, try getting a coffee maker with a timer, ensuring that you'll wake up to the smell of freshly made coffee. Preparing breakfast food and ingredients at night would also make it easier for you to start cooking a healthy and delicious meal in the morning.

Cheese Works

This is a fun thing to try! So let's say the room is too cold and your cheapskate boss won't let you touch the thermostat. Try putting a block of cheese on top of the device and it will be fooled into thinking that the room is actually colder than it actually is. Hence, the temperature is automatically adjusted, giving you a warmer and more comfortable atmosphere.

Surround Yourself with Yellow

Ever wondered why Facebook is colored blue? Studies suggest that this color is the most relaxing for people so when using Facebook, you tend to relax and spend lots of time on the website. On the other side of the spectrum, there's the color yellow that can help increase your productivity. The color closely resembles the brightness of the sun, which fools the body into producing melatonin. This basically stops you from being sleepy in the middle of the afternoon, allowing you to focus more on the job and less on the bed.

Baby Animals are the Answer

Now we know why the internet is littered with images of cute baby animals. It actually produces productivity – according to a study done by the Hiroshima University. Apparently, cute baby animals can give you a buzz that restores your energy and relaxes the mind, making you ready for work. With just one minute of scrolling through pictures of cats sitting in bowls, you'd be able to increase productivity by up to 44 percent...

Commute

Taking your car might be more convenient, but commuting to work actually makes it easier for you to face the day. Instead of driving, you can rearrange your schedule for the next 8 hours, making sure that all your papers are in order and answering emails through your phone. Simply put, commuting lets you focus on those "little things" that make you ready for the "big things" in the office.

Get to Work Early

Getting to work early won't just impress the boss; it would also make your whole day more productive. First off, being early means you'll miss the morning rush hour which can be—let's face it—very annoying. Upon reaching the office, there would be zero colleagues around, letting you avoid the typical small talk in the morning. With zero stress and distractions, you'd be in a prime mindset to do whatever needs to be done and get the job finished ahead of schedule. Even better, that means you'd be finished earlier so you can get out of the office quickly and avoid the usual 5:30 PM rush.

Change Your Surroundings

Is it possible to bring your work somewhere else? Like the best coffee shop near you? Believe it or not, some people actually get a boost in productivity when around other people. The buzz of the noise and activity provides them with a burst of energy that you just can't find in the stale surroundings of the office. Of course, this might not work for everyone so try experimenting on your surroundings to find out which setting gives you the most buzz.

Bribe Yourself

Do you need to finish reading a long and boring report? Put a (healthy) snack at the end of each page and eat it when you read that specific page. You'll find yourself becoming more enthusiastic with the reading process.

Keep Plants Nearby

Even if it's just a small pot of green, plants can actually work wonders for your concentration. This has been proven after two studies performed in 2011 and 2013. According to psychologists from the University of Michigan, plants are part of the "attention restoration theory" which basically means it restores your focus on the work with just one quick glimpse. Don't forget that the green color of plants is also excellent for the eyes so you're basically "refreshing" your mind and vision through a simple plant. With you practically rejuvenated, your work productivity should increase.

Nap a Little

Google's main office actually has a nap room where employees can take a well-deserved snooze. Some might think this defeats productivity but studies reveal that a nap – when done at the right time – actually revitalizes your physical and mental energy bar. Ever taken a nap in the afternoon and woke up feeling like you can take over the world? That's it! Of course, optimum napping time is different for everyone, although studies show that generally, it's somewhere within the vicinity of 2PM. You'll find that someone ingeniously crafted a nap wheel for this, letting you calculate your optimum napping time, depending on what time you sleep and what time you wake up. Of course, you can always follow what your body dictates and nap when you're feeling drowsy.

Big Tasks in the Morning

Studies reveal that the morning is your most productive time yet. Maybe it has something to do with waking up from a long and satisfying rest. No matter the reason, try scheduling your biggest, worst and usually most important tasks in the morning. You'll find that not only do you have more energy during the early hours, but your mind is also sharper and more creative. We're not just talking about eight, nine, or ten in the morning, however. If you wake up around 6AM, you'll notice that you're practically bursting with energy around 6:30AM. Of course, this might not be true for everyone – but it's certainly worth a try!

Binaural Beats

Ever heard of binaural beats? They've been proven to help with concentration, creating a more productive workplace for you. Try downloading one online and see if it works for you.

Any Music Works

Binaural beats are great – but the truth is that every type of music works in boosting your productivity. According to studies, listening to music you like helps you finish tasks faster. This is especially true if you're not particularly fond of the job you're doing. Music essentially helps "entertain" you while performing laborious or boring tasks, making the whole job seem easier.

Make a To-Do List (seriously)

Now, this one is up for debate so you might want to test each method out before making a decision. First off, create a to-do list for the day, scheduling the worst tasks in the morning when your energy is at its highest. Stick to this to-do list and apply the Seinfeld approach by putting a big fat red check beside every task you finish. Period.

Take a Computer Break

The problem with computers is that even though they increase productivity, they also decrease it. How many times have you browsed through your Facebook or Twitter account when you're supposed to be doing work? With "fun" websites so easily accessible, it's very common to have multiple tabs open in your window. Hence, if you've decided you need a "break" from work, try standing up from the desk and stretching your legs. This would help clear your head, give you the break you want, and even burn some calories along the way!

Anti-Distraction Software

Get some help from programs available for free. A good example is JDarkRoom, which basically obliterates all possible distractions from your monitor. Instead, the screen is filled by a completely white page where you can write your report. The taskbar, start icon and others are papered over by the document, allowing you to completely focus on what's important.

Download Evernote

Evernote is an application that helps you stay organized. Most people only use it to take notes, but there's actually so much more that can be done with this program. You can try creating lots of notebooks and notes, linking them together and creating a whole system of pages that help you keep track of information you need. Perhaps one of the best features of the program is the Web Clipper, which lets you save articles from the internet, add them to existing notes and even make notes of them so that you don't forget anything! Have fun and explore with this program.

Meal Planning

Indecisiveness is one of the most common reasons for procrastination – so why not remove the option when you can? Plan your meals ahead of schedule so that you know exactly what you're eating for the day. If you love to cook, this means having all the important ingredients in the pantry, removing the need for a time-wasting shopping expedition.

Carry a Notebook and Pen Around (All. The. Time.)

Do you get ideas in your head that constantly nag and distract you throughout the day? Ideas like these might be excellent, but they can push you to procrastinate, bumping out all the concentration you have for the job. Get rid of all these nagging by writing all those thoughts and "light bulbs" in a notebook you always keep handy. After writing them down, your subconscious should feel content so that you can focus on the work again. At the end of the day, you can visit the notebook again and get to work on your bright ideas!

Break the TV Habit

According to studies, the typical American spends around 9 years out of a 65-year life span watching television. This basically boil down to 4 hours each day – but imagine how long it really is when you look at the big picture. Turn off the TV now and start doing something else. Read a good book, for example. Not only will you become more productive, you'd also find yourself saving on electricity!

Blog It

Blog what you do, your goals, what you've been doing to achieve them, and how you're faring so far. The incentive of being able to chronicle your "adventures" should be able to push you towards productivity. For some people, knowing that others are reading their work is an excellent inducer. Of course, this might not work for everyone and in some cases, you might consider it additional work rather than fun.

Sleep Well

Well, duh. Sleep has long been strongly advised to increase productivity and improve overall health. Unfortunately, a lot of people are still ignoring this fact, so please—try to get a good eight hours of sleep every night.

Clean Up!

OK, so opinions for this one are also divided. Basically, the idea is to get rid of any clutter on your desk before starting work. With a clean and orderly desk, there's really nothing else for you to do but focus on the work. Of course, don't forget the Einstein quote: 'If a cluttered desk is a sign of a cluttered mind, of what, then, is an empty desk a sign?' So basically, what you can do is clean your desk but don't leave it completely devoid of anything. For some people, a stack of paperwork on their desk helps to constantly remind them that there's still work to be done. Hence, this is really a judgment call on your part. My advice – remove the clutter and see what happens.

The Email Reverse Psychology

Ever want someone to read your email immediately? Use the reverse psychology trick! After sending them the mail, follow it up with another mail bearing the subject: PLS DON'T READ PREVIOUS EMAIL. IT WAS SENT IN ERROR. Yup, do it in all caps to really get the reader's attention. You'll find that this would make them very curious about the email's content.

Work in Sprints

Work shouldn't be a marathon that keeps you sitting on your chair for six long hours at a time. Instead, you should approach it in sprints, perhaps spending two hours at a time and then taking a quick break to refresh yourself. Note, though, that your "refreshment" of choice should not be done by clicking through your social media account. Instead, stand up, walk around, stretch a little or even grab a cup of water. A few minutes away from the computer would give you that necessary recharge to keep on working.

Move Around and Workout

Studies reveal that exercise can help increase your productivity, increase concentration, and improve your energy. It probably has something to do with exercise improving blood flow and oxygen in the body. We're not just talking about morning exercises, although that's definitely a good thing. Instead, try to insert some workouts during your lunch hour or even the 15-minute break. Even just walking in place or light stretching can turn you into a whole new person.

Turn your Phone Off

OK, so maybe turning your phone off all the way is not necessary. However, you can try locking it up in the drawer (or just putting it into flight mode) to prevent yourself from checking it every few minutes.

Second Monitor

Now this might seem irrational, but a second monitor can actually make it easier for you to work. Employees notice that switching from one window to another actually makes it harder for them to concentrate on what they're doing. With a second monitor, however, it seems as though the whole process has just become way easier, not to mention easier on the eyes. Also, monitors today have become cheaper so this shouldn't dent your bank account too much.

Donuts Fix Everything

Running late and you just know everyone is going to welcome you with bad looks in the office? You can't really blame them, especially since they've been ahead of you. You know what you can do, though? Donuts! A box of donuts may not completely wipe off the frown on their faces, but they shouldn't give you a hard time with your lateness. After all, a happy office is a productive office. Don't do it again, though – buying 54 donuts every day can be quite expensive.

Herbs are the Answer

Aside from sounds and visual elements, another factor that deeply affects work productivity is the smell. If you're in an environment where the smell is far from pleasant, chances are you wouldn't be in your full capacity when working. Don't grab the air freshener, though. This will only make things worse because the slight chemical smell is an even bigger distraction. Instead, go to the local greenhouse and purchase an herb plant – preferably one with a strong smell. Put it beside the office desk and you should get that clean, fresh smell of the outdoors all day long. Some of the best plants for this job are mint, basil, rosemary and lavender.

Pomodoro Method

The Pomodoro technique is very simple to do and can increase your focus and productivity significantly during the day. Basically, just set a timer for 25 minutes and commit yourself to working during that time. You don't have to finish the task within those 25 minutes; you just have to make sure that all those minutes are used productively. When you're done, take a 5-minute break; you've earned it! Repeat the process over and over again until the day is done. You can also try giving yourself a longer 15-minute break after four or five 25-minute cycles.

Batch 'Em Up

Try to batch up your tasks or work in chunks for the smaller jobs that necessitate a few minutes of your time. For example, schedule your email checks, messenger checks and updates together, allowing you to get those things out of the way immediately. With that gone, you can now focus on the biggest and most important tasks of the day.

Just Work Wednesdays

Some companies also call them "No Meeting Tuesdays" which basically means that there is zero chance of a meeting being called for in the company boardroom. This simple policy lets everyone know that the day is purely dedicated to work which means that they don't have to worry about any distractions. Why Wednesday? Any day could work, but Wednesday is the optimum day because it is smack in the middle of the week when the employees are best primed for work.

Block Websites

So let's say you just can't help yourself from constantly checking your Facebook and Twitter account. There are ways to temporarily block these websites and stop you from procrastinating your day away. Some programs that can help include LeechBlock, Focus Booster, Self Control, Nanny for Google Chrome, Keep Me Out, and StayFocused.

and StayFocused.

Pareto's Law

Pareto's Law states that 20% of your inputs lead to 80% of the outputs. That means that for every 10 things that you do, even just doing 2 of those would give more than half of the results you want. Sound confusing? Alright, let's keep it simple. Before the day starts, think about the top three things you need to do in order to reach your goals for the day. By staying focused on those three things, you'd find yourself reaching 100% productivity!

Walking Meetings

Have walking meetings! It not only saves time but the walk actually helps stimulate the mind, allowing you to come up with better ideas.

Give yourself a bedtime

A part of growing up was not having to listen to your parents say 'lights out,' when you can think of a million and one things that you'd rather be doing than sleeping. However, as we get older, we lose out on sleeping time, thinking about our work-day and all the things that need to be done tomorrow. Of course, most of the time, rather than actually getting work done, we're procrastinating. Setting a bedtime, will limit the amount of procrastination you get done and add to the amount of rejuvenating sleep you're able to accomplish.

Skip the news until the important tasks have been taken care of

Most people like to check up on the world first thing in the morning. Friends on Facebook, happenings in the newspaper, stories on the radio, they're often the first things that people turn to when they awake (outside of a cup of coffee).

This, unfortunately, leads to a buildup in interest. One fun post means that you've got to read another and one interesting story leads to you scouring the internet for more details.

Getting your important tasks done first and saving the news until lunch time will mean that you get a lot done early in the morning, before the day slowly but surely fades away. Plus, it gives you something to look forward to and the faster you work, the faster you get to see what happened in the hours the internet hadn't been your main focus.

Plan meals ahead

The more time you take flipping through the internet for lunch ideas or comparing what you had last week for dinner, the more time you'll waste just thinking about what you want to eat. Of course it may not seem like you're putting that much time into deciding on meals, however, add this up over the course of a month and you'll more than likely have wasted hours. Include your lunch and dinner plans on your calendar and never have to spend another minute (outside of calendar prep time) thinking about what you want to eat for lunch. The longer you keep up with this, the easier it will be to stick to what your calendar says.

Don't be afraid to say 'NO'

This can be an exceptionally hard one. If you're the kind of person who pushes of important tasks to please others then you're doing it all wrong. Always prioritize and think about how going to the movies, out for a drink after work or having a long lunch will affect your productivity. A nice let down is always better than being **in a rut because you said 'yes' when you should have said 'no'.**

If you're going to procrastinate, do so with a purpose

If you're stuck on a task and procrastinating is inevitable, you'll want to make sure that your procrastination counts. Rather than staring out the window, refreshing Facebook for the millionth time or finding new things to 'Pin', create a list of productive things you can do when you just can't force yourself to work on the task you should be completed. This can include anything from cleaning out your inbox to replying to emails and from shredding unnecessary paperwork to creating your lunch list.

Trick yourself

Set deadlines a day or two earlier. This is something that works wonders. Even though in the beginning you'll know that you still have a day or two to turn in 'the paperwork' or 'project', as you keep up with this hack, your brain will readjust and you'll start believing in these deadlines and ensuring that you get the work done by the set deadline rather than the actual deadline.

No more multitasking

The more you multitask, the less focus you will have and the more time it will actually take you to get your work done. Instead, you want to dedicate all your focus to one project, and in doing so, you'll work faster and more seamlessly.

Giving your all to one task at a time will definitely work to improve your productivity and eliminate unnecessary mistakes. Especially when working with something potentially dangerous, you'll want to skip the multitasking and channel your focus in one direction.

Get to the point

When writing emails, rather than including lots of unnecessary mumbo jumbo, you want to get right to the point. Trying to get your point across in 5 sentences or less will save you lots of time to answer even more emails and complete other necessary tasks.

HEALTH

Health hacks have been around for years, often passed down to us by our elders. When I was growing up, my grandmother would offer her advice on how to handle some of these problems, and thought she had no idea what she was talking about because the remedies seemed a bit silly. I chalked them up to old wives' tales, but as it turned out, she was quite right.

Let's take a look at some hacks that can solve every day, minor health issues. Using these solutions will make your life so much easier!

1. Cure a Headache Without a Pain Reliever. One of the most common reasons people get headaches is due to dehydration. The next time you get a headache, instead of reaching for acetaminophen or ibuprofen, reach for Gatorade.

Consuming two glasses of Gatorade will stop your headache quickly, and will actually address the reason why you got a headache in the first place rather than just mask the pain. The electrolytes and carbohydrates in the Gatorade allow the fluid to be absorbed more efficiently in your body than just drinking water, instantly rehydrating you.

2. Relieve Minor Sunburns Naturally. If you have a minor sunburn and don't have any aloe vera, you can relieve your burn by applying tea bags to your skin. Soak black tea bags in warm water. Drain some of the excess water from the tea bags and place them in your freezer for 20 minutes.

Apply the chilled tea bags directly to your sunburn. The tea's tannins and anti-inflammatory properties will help soothe your skin and activate the healing process quickly. If you don't have black tea in your home, you can substitute chamomile tea.

3. Sleep Smarter. We all know that getting quality sleep for 8 hours a night maximizes our effectiveness and mental state the following day. Sometimes it's hard to get the full 8 hours, but let's look at the most effective ways you can get the best quality of sleep.

Stop drinking beverages with caffeine in them at least six hours before you go to bed. Shut off your television and stop looking at "screens" (computer, phone, etc.) an hour before you go to bed. The release of melatonin helps you fall asleep at night and it has been proven that looking at the light on our gadget screens actually suppresses that natural release.

Avoid hitting your snooze button, as it causes your REM sleep to be disrupted, resulting in you feeling even more tired. If you are tempted to hit the snooze button like I often am, move your alarm so you are forced to get out of bed and shut it off.

4. Make Your Own Flexible Ice Pack. Instead of spending $10-$15 to purchase an ice pack at your local pharmacy, you can make one with ingredients you already have at home. Simply take a gallon zip top bag and fill with three parts water to one part rubbing alcohol and place it in your freezer.

The alcohol will prevent the water from completely freezing and will allow the mixture to be flexible for better application. Once you are ready to use it, take it out of your freezer and wrap in a towel and apply to the affected area.

5. Soothe a Sore Throat Naturally. If you have a sore throat or a persistent cough you can calm it down with items you have at home in your pantry. Create a soothing syrup by combining a ¼ teaspoon of cayenne pepper, 1 teaspoon of apple cider vinegar, 1 tablespoon of honey and 2 tablespoons of water. Mix together until you have a thin, smooth consistency and drink.

6. Ease Bloating. We've all experienced the discomfort of bloating when eating more than we should have at a delicious meal. When our body breaks down food, some carbohydrates cannot be digested in the small intestine, so it moves along to our large intestine in its undigested form. This causes gas to build, resulting in the body feeling bloated.

Drinking a few cups of dandelion tea will help purge excess water in your body and will stimulate bile that will cause the undigested food in your large intestine to break down quickly, relieving the bloat.

7. Banish Toenail Fungus. Fungal infections under your toenails can be treated effectively with Listerine. You can soak your feet in Listerine twice a day until the infection clears up, or you can apply a small amount of Listerine directly to the affected area twice a day with a Q-Tip or a small brush.

You can also mix one part Listerine and one part white vinegar and soak your feet in that mixture. The antiseptic properties in Listerine will help disinfect your toenails and the white vinegar will make the environment too acidic for the fungi. This acidic environment kills off the fungi.

8. Stop Ice Cream Headaches. Ice cream headaches, often called "brain freeze" occurs when we eat something cold too fast. When the roof of our mouth feels the cold sensation, it causes a dilation of the blood vessels in our head, which causes a sharp cold headache.

When you feel the headache start, press your tongue on the roof of your mouth (this is where the nerve center is located that is causing your blood vessels to enlarge and cause the headache) this will soothe the nerves and the heat from your tongue will signal to the brain that it isn't as cold.

HACKS FOR THE OFFICE

Re-record voicemail

If you're having a busy day returning phone calls or getting in touch with clients and get the 'please record your message after the beep,' but for some reason your speech fails you and the message doesn't come out just right, you can re-record. By pressing the # symbol on your phone, you can erase your message and re-record.

Tired of overspending on coffee, but still want more?

Rather than ordering a medium in a medium cup, order a medium coffee in a large cup. Your barrister will more than likely get the measurements wrong and end up giving you an Extra Medium coffee.

Paper cuts don't have to ruin your day

If you're flipping through papers too fast and ended up with one of those really annoying and surprisingly excruciating paper cuts, get out your chap stick and offer yourself an immediate relief from the pain.

Bye-bye telemarketers

If your office phone is subject to an influx of telemarketer calls on a regular basis, hit the 9 while in the call and the phone number will be moved to the don't call list.

More ink from no ink

In the middle of printing an important document and your computer tells you you're out of ink? There's no need to worry because there's still more ink in your cartridge. To retrieve it, remove the cartridge, get a pointy item like a paperclip (when unfolded) or a pin, poke the reset button, plug your cartridge back in and you'll notice that your ink wasn't empty after all.

IPad for iPhone

If you're in a hurry to get your phone charged and you've got both an iPhone and an iPad, use your iPad charger for your iPhone and charge up in rapid speed. It may sound a bit silly, but it really does work.

Good battery? Bad battery?

To check if your battery has still got some life in it, bounce it on the ground from about 6 inches. If it falls flat after a single bounce, it' still good. More bounces mean that they've reached the end or are approaching the end.

Get more life out of your laptop battery

To increase the life of your laptop battery, rather than charging to 100%, charge to 80%.

Dropped you phone in water?

Fill a bowl with rice and submerge your phone in the bowl. Leave the phone in the rice for about a day to allow the rice to absorb the moisture from your phone.

Clean keyboard

Use tape or Blu-tack to get to those hard to reach spaces on your keyboard and get rid of all the crumbs and dust that your keyboard has been hoarding.

Headphone holder

Attach a paperclip to the side of your desk and wrap your headphones around it when not in use.

ORGANIZATION

I love organization hacks because it saves me time and saves me the stress of frantically trying to find something that is buried in a mess. Minimalists teach that having an organized, clean home creates a more organized mind. Let's take a look at some organization tricks that will save you time, space and money.

An unorganized house, a stuffy room, or a cluttered environment not only decreases productivity and make things more difficult to find, but they also cause unnecessary stress. Everything in the world, alive or dead, has an energy. In a room that is full of clutter and not properly organized, the energy will weigh you down, stress you, decrease your quality of life, and may even cause depression. So, it is important to keep everything organized to simplify your life. Following are some life hacks that will help you get more organized.

1. Create Drawer Dividers. You can easily de-clutter a junk drawer by cutting up shoeboxes or cereal boxes and creating little compartments inside a drawer. I measure my boxes out so that the depth of each box is slightly shorter than the depth of the drawer, then I cover the boxes with pretty, coordinating wrapping paper to spruce it up.

I've de-cluttered junk drawers, organized my clothes in my dresser and have organized toiletries in the bathroom using this method. I've often received compliments on where I "bought" my drawer dividers. You can use this organization technique for categorizing makeup and crafts as well.

2. Organize Your Jewelry. I can't tell you how many times I've searched for a specific piece of jewelry last minute and couldn't find it. I developed a system that really works and that has prevented necklaces and bracelets from getting tangled. Take a couple of glass beer bottles and rinse them thoroughly and allow them to dry completely. Cover each bottle with wrapping paper or craft paper (or don't – it's up to you!). Stack your bracelets around the bottle for easy storage.

If you don't have any beer bottles, you can also use a paper towel holder. For necklaces and dangle earrings, buy an inexpensive cork board and insert pins into the cork. Hang your necklaces and dangle earrings from the pins.

3. Make a Plastic Bag Dispenser. We all save our plastic bags from our trips from the grocery store. I used to bunch them all up and toss them into one bag and shove them in the pantry. Of course, it was always a pain to dig through the big bag of crumpled plastic bags when I needed one, so I created a bag dispenser. Take a tissue box that is empty and neatly fold the plastic bags so they naturally "dispense" through the top of the tissue box when the one before is pulled out.

4. Use a Cloth Shoe Rack to Organize Cleaning Products. We've all had to go digging under our kitchen or bathroom sink looking for a specific cleaner to clean up a mess. Instead of having to dig through the mess, hang a cloth shoe rack over the back of your laundry room door and store all your household cleaners in each compartment. I like organizing my types of cleaners so I can easily find them.

5. Build a Scarf Hanger. To easily consolidate all your scarves, keep them all on one hanger. Take a sturdy hanger (preferably wood) and loop shower curtain rings through the bottom part of the hanger, so you have a line of rings along the bottom. Put one scarf in each ring. You should easily be able to fit 12-15 scarves on one hanger.

6. Box Your Batteries. If rummaging through a junk drawer trying to locate the right battery size is not your idea of fun, organize all your batteries in a tackle box. Store your batteries by size in their own compartments so the next time you need to find a battery quickly, it's super easy.

7. Keep Cords from Being Out of Control. We've all seen, and perhaps experienced in our own homes, the rat's nest of cords behind the entertainment center. You can keep the excess cord lengths in check by reusing the cardboard toilet tissue rolls as sleeves to contain neatly folded excess cord. You can also use this method to keep extension cords neatly folded up and in the toilet roll sleeve. If you don't like using cardboard for your cords, fold them the same way, then fasten together with wire twist ties.

8. Fashion Your Own Can Dispenser. Storing your canned goods in one place in your pantry will allow for better storage and utilization of space. Take a few empty soda can holder/dispensers (the ones that usually hold 12 cans) and decorate them with craft paper or wrapping paper. Categorize by soups, beans, canned protein, etc. and store in each box for easy storage and access.

9. You can use nail polish to mark your keys and keep them organized. Assign each color to a room, or organize as you please.

10. To create more space in a drawer and to find your shirts more easily, instead of laying them over one another after folding them, place them vertically. This way you can easily see them all and pick the one you want, instead of pulling one out from under the bundle and messing the others up.

11. You can organize your plastic bags by putting them inside a tissue box; remove one as needed, just like pulling out a tissue.

12. The cut-off spot on sticky tapes is difficult to find. Instead of looking around the tape to find the cut-off spot each time you need to use the tape, use a paper clip to hold the cut-off spot instead.

13. The old door knobs can be installed in the bathroom or kitchen walls for hanging towels.

14. Paper towel holders can be used for hanging wristbands, watches, bracelets, and even rings.

15. You can use your old drawers and paint, modify, or decorate them, and use them as shelves.

16. You can install wine racks in the shower room to hold several towels at the same time.

17. The hanging shoe racks can also be used in the bathroom, kitchen, or office for storing supplies. The pockets can hold toiletries, office supplies, eatables, etc.

18. To save space in the room, you can hang your ironing board on coat hangers.

19. You can install an extra shower curtain rod in your bathroom to hang your loofahs and other bathroom items.

20. Use shower hooks to hang your pants, jeans, shorts, etc. in the closet. They will be easier to remove, browse through, and hang back.

21. A shoe rack can also be used for holding bottles and small containers in place.

22. Paper clips can be used for keeping the cables organized.

23. The tabs from soda cans can be used to offset hangers and create more space in the closet.

24. Use the empty toilet paper rolls to store wires, cords, and cables in them. It will make it easy for you to store them in a box without having to worry about them getting tangled or intertwined.

25. Hair clips can be used to organize headphones, earphones, and other long wires and cords.

26. To store the lids of Tupperware, use an old CD rack or tower.

27. Create more space in your room by using the back of your door. Use a door storage organizer, shoe holder, or a shelf to utilize the space.

28. Cereal boxes can be cut, wrapped, decorated, and used for organizing the drawers.

29. Use hidden drawers to utilize the extra space you have under your bed.

30. Reuse tin cans for storing your art or office supplies, like pens, colors, crayons, etc.

31. When storing boxes, label them. Though this does not seem important when storing them, it saves a lot of time when you need to retrieve them.

32. Use double sided sticky tapes and fix them on the edges of your coffee table. Stick the remotes on them, pull them off when you need them, and stick them back after use. Do this and you will never lose your remotes again.

33. Use a paint palette for your jewelry. Keep a pair in each section and they will always be organized and easy to find.

34. Attach a Velcro strip to your electronic machines and their cords, and stick the cords back on the machine after use.

35. Curtain rods can be installed under the sink for hanging bottles and creating more storage space.

36. Use a wine rack and add some tin cans or plastic containers to store art supplies in an organized way.

37. To label the cords of computer like mouse, keyboard, speakers, printer, scanner, etc., or the cords of TV, DVD, etc., use bread clips. It will make it easy for you to identify them if you need to switch or replace them.

38. Tackle boxes can be used to keep tiny miscellaneous items, like batteries, cells, pins, etc. organized.

LIFE HACKS FOR YOUR HOME

More often than not, you have more than enough things on your hands when you come home from work. The checklist of things to do never seems to be completed. When you arrive from your work, you'd probably prioritize rest over the completion of household tasks and chores. However, if you do this often, your house is probably a huge mess by now!

After a hard day's work, it can be nearly impossible to find the energy to make sure that your home is neat and clean. But with determination and the help of life hacks, you will be able to magically complete your tasks in no time. If you are familiar with life hacks techniques and methods, you will easily be able to complete your tasks without draining your energy.

Imagine how easy your life would be if you are more efficient in doing the laundry and cleaning the home. You will have more time to do the things you actually want to do. In addition to this, you can spend more time bonding with your family.

There are many life hacks that can be put to use around your house. There are tricks that are applicable in your living room, kitchen, laundry, bedroom, bathroom, backyard/front lawn, and garage. Wherever you use these hacks, you will get amazing results for organizing and cleaning in a better way. The solution to your problems is within your reach!

So what is next? Hacks to use at home. Here are some quick tips to make your life easier and much more manageable.

Life Hacks for Your Living Room

Your living room needs to look good because this is where you will entertain guests and visitors. Here are ideas that can help you be proud of our own living room. As the name implies, a living room is a place for the family to share time together.

Sometimes you watch a movie or a TV program, other times the room is used for board games or TV games. It is also a place for informal get-togethers with friends and family. So this is a versatile room and sees a lot of traffic.

Because of the diverse uses of this room it needs to be functional, properly spaced and have ample storage for everything that is needed in the room.

Quick hacks:

1. Remove the clutter. Get as much as possible off the floor to make cleaning fast and easy. Remember this room sees a lot of traffic.

2. Install castors or wheels to the coffee table, ottomans and pieces of furniture that you need to move around.

3. Install drawers or baskets into the coffee table to house items that you need every day, for example, remote controls, TV guides and coasters.

4. Install shelving for books, games, DVDs and other dust gathering items. Bonus points for installing doors to the shelves. Take time to sort the books and DVDs to find your favorites quickly! If guests arrive, close the doors and the room will be instantly neat.

5. Use baskets (in the coffee table or shelving) to group common things together. This could be a box of candles, platters for snacks, toys, extra batteries, globes, or even your knitting. Now you only need to take one container out and have everything ready for a specific function.

6. Instead of hanging a lot of pictures in frames, opt for very narrow floating shelves do display your photos. Use these to display other items as well.

7. Use old crates (similar or various sizes) as a wall mounted display shelves. To extra depth to the room, install mirrors on the bottoms of the crates.

8. Lighting is very important in this room. Get rid of the single source of light in the center of the ceiling and install sets of low-voltage LED down-lighters. Wire them to switch them on in sets: Switch all of them on when hosting a get together, but only one set when you watch TV. Not only will you save money, but flush-mount down-lighters do not gather dust.

9. Use your wall space in a clever way. Install a large mirror on a wall to make the space look bigger. If you need extra light or lights that form part of the décor, cut an interesting shaped lamp in two and wall mount for both light and décor.

10. If you only use your TV occasionally, wall mount the unit and cover it with a framed picture that is hinged on one side. Neatly tie the cables together and hide them behind a vase, a box or freestanding photo frame.

11. Over the years, your walls might start to smell like food, cigarettes, or an "old house." The problem could get even worse if you have a pet. It can be hard to get rid of the animal smell when it sticks to the wall. You don't need to spend a fortune on expensive chemicals. Just wipe down walls and furniture with a mixture of one part white vinegar and eight parts water to remove bad odors from your home.

12. Carpets are beautiful and elegant. However, trying to maintain them involves a lot of work Here are a few hacks that could make your life significantly easier.

> 1. Placing furniture on your carpet will cause them to have dents. Don't stress about this! Simply rub the unsightly parts with a cube of ice. Finally, pat with a cloth, and your carpet or rug will be as good as new.

> 2. Do you have pets or children who cause your rugs to move? In order to keep your rug or carpet in place, attach a Velcro strip on the carpet and a Velcro strip on the floor. This little trick will keep the rug in place.

13. You'll be surprised to know that food and drinks can be used for furniture maintenance. Wooden furniture is beautiful, and it will give your living room a vintage look. However, you need to exert extra effort if you want your wooden furniture to look good.

1. You can use flat beer to clean your furniture. All you have to do is pour beer on a soft cloth and simply wipe it down the wooden furniture. This simple process will help restore the color of your furniture.

2. If your furniture has damages and scratches, you will find the unlikely solution to your problem in the form of a walnut. Simply rub a walnut on the surface of the furniture so that the walnut oil could help restore the flawless look of your wooden furniture.

Life Hacks for Your Kitchen and Laundry

Cleaning the kitchen and doing the laundry can be two of the most taxing things that you need to do in order to maintain your home. Here are some tips that can help make your tasks easier.

For Kitchen-

Cleaning the kitchen can be such a difficult challenge. You'll need to clean your sink, floor, and all the cabinets. On top of these, you also have to take care of the eating and cooking utensils. If you don't use life hacks, it might take you forever to clean the kitchen. Here are some handy tips that you can use to keep your kitchen tidy.

Cleaning your stove top can really be difficult, because it is often prone to so many spills and stuck-on messes. You don't have to buy expensive solutions to get the job done. With this life hack, cleaning your stove will be significantly easier! Combine one tablespoon of salt with one tablespoon of baking soda and one tablespoon of water. Mix the paste together. Use the mixture like an ordinary cleaner, and scrub away!

You can easily clean stains on coffee and tea mugs, by rubbing them with lemon peel and salt. This combination is powerful against dirt and stains.

If you use a blender or a food processor, you don't need to scrub and wash the container. Simply "blend" or "process" a few drops of dishwashing liquid along with half a cup of water. Let the machine clean itself for you! You don't need to exert effort anymore. All you have to do is press a button.

A kitchen is the heart of any home. Most modern homes in cities have very small kitchens, so you have to really think about the space to optimize every available nook and cranny.

A lot of work gets done in the kitchen and it should be ready at any time of the day. Everything that you do to make your life a little easier in this room will save you heaps of time and effort. Cooking only becomes a drag if you have to fight your way around the kitchen. Here are some simple and more involved things to make the kitchen a "healthy" heart of the home.

1. A fire blanket and/or fire extinguisher is a must in every kitchen. Make sure everybody in the house knows how to use them.

2. Because you are working with food and beverages the kitchen should always be clean. To make this possible, try to clear up as much counter space as possible. If an appliance is used only occasionally, pack it into the back of a cupboard or even in the pantry or attic.

3. Install electrical outlets under the top cupboards to get electrical cords out of the way.

4. You can change your kitchen as the seasons change – in the same way as you change your clothing cupboards. Replace the ice cream maker with the crockpot in winter, or swop your soup bowls for salad bowls in the summer. Most of the time it is just a matter of repacking a cupboard.

5. Invest in covers for all your appliances that stand in the open. It will keep them clean, and if you make a mess in the kitchen it is easier to put the covers in the wash than to clean every appliance.

6. Most of the action takes place around the oven, stove or hob. Make sure that all the utensils, pots and pans are within easy reach so that you do not have to run around looking for things.

7. If you are considering remodeling your kitchen, opt for drawer units for all the floor-standing units. It is very difficult to find a pack or clean things in floor

cupboards. This is especially true for things that land up at the back. Drawers should pull out all the way so that you can see everything at once glance. The drawer units work well if the sizes of the drawers are not all the same. Use pot drawers at the bottom for pots, mixing bowls, appliances and tall food ingredients. Use medium drawers for crockery, dinner service, condiments, glasses and cooking utensils. Use shallow drawers for cutlery, spices and cups. If you like baking, install 7 or 8 shallow drawers in the counter for all your baking tools, cookie cutters, pans, icing bits and pieces as well as all the food coloring, essence, palette knives and cake boards. By having a lot of shallow drawers, nothing lies on top of each other and everything is visible when you need something.

8. Convert your kick plates under the cupboards to either drawers or boxes to stand on to reach the top cupboards.

9. Lift your dishwasher by 9 to 12 inches by placing it on a little cupboard with a single drawer. Store dishwashing soap, cleaning chemicals or rags in this drawer. By lifting the dishwasher, you will save your back when loading and unloading dishes. This is very important if you consider that the heaviest items are normally at the bottom of the appliance.

10. Some houses have a dining room next to the kitchen. If you hardly ever use your dining room, break out the wall between the kitchen and dining room and enlarge your kitchen. You might even have space for a colorful couch in your new kitchen for your guests to relax on while you are preparing food.

11. If your sink is clogged, you can use Alka-Seltzer tablets to unclog the drains. If you want to prevent glasses & silverware from breaking, use rubber bands to keep them in place. You can also put old newspapers at the bottom of the trash bag in the bin to absorb leftover food juices and keep your trash cans clean and dry. This will prevent any sort of liquid from creating a mess in your kitchen.

For Laundry and Closets

Closets are great for storage. Here are a few hacks to use the space in a clever way.

1. If you have fixed shelves in a closet, remove the shelving and either drill holes for shelving supports from the bottom to the top, or install metal shelving strips to make all the shelves adjustable. Most of the wasted space in a closet can be attributed to the empty space between the top of items and the bottom of the next shelf. You might even be able to add a couple of shelves by going for an adjustable solution. (If you cannot match the old shelving, cover all the shelves with washable wallpaper.)

2. You can also convert existing shelves into pullout units so better access the items on the shelf. Cut off the edge of the shelves to accommodate the runners and add a narrow frame around the edges to prevent items from falling off. The frame will also give you a place to grip the shelf for pulling it out.

3. Install a slim bookcase in the center of a closet for racks and run rods between the bookcase and walls for hanging clothes. The rods will also help to stabilize the shelves.

4. If you need to store a lot of small items in a closet, group them together in boxes, baskets of plastic containers. Not only will you find things quickly, but your closet will look organized.

5. Create extra space in your closets by installing rods on the inside of the doors. Use these to scarves, ties, hats, belts or any other slim items.

Laundry rooms should be filled with clean smells, lots of light and with as many things as possible to make laundry day a breeze.

1. Build a closet next to or around your appliances. Use the closet to sort every-thing you might need in the laundry. Top shelves in the closet can also house extra linen for the house, tablecloths, napkins and even clothes that need mending.

2. If you are building a closet, make a list of all the items that need to be stored. Remember to create a thin, but tall space for the ironing board, broom and mops.

3. Attach magnets to the corners of a quilted ironing board cover and frappe it over your drier for a quick place to iron a shirt or dress before you go out. No need to lug out the ironing board.

4. Make your own reusable dryer sheets by combining 1/2 cup of vinegar and 8 drops tea tree or other essential oil. Cut up some old T-shirts or cotton cloth and sprinkle the mix over (do not soak). Store in an airtight mason jar. When needed remove from the jar, squeeze out over the jar and pop into the drier. When you are done, place at the bottom of the jar again.

5. Install a shelf over the drier. Not only is it a place for storage, but you can sus-pend a rod from the bottom of the shelf to store extra hangers, or to hang up clothes as you take them out of the drier.

6. A dirty washing machine cannot clean your clothes. Clean your washing machine by running a hot water cycle with 2 cups of vinegar and 1 cup of baking soda in the drum. Remember to remove the soap dispenser and give it a good scrub with an old toothbrush. While you are cleaning the machine check and clean all the filters as well. Repeat this at least twice a year to keep your machine running optimally.

7. Lift your front loading washing machine and dryer about 12 inches from the floor by building a sturdy wooden box for them to stand on. This will make loading and unloading easy on your back, and you can use the space below them for stor-age baskets to store any of the many things you need in a laundry.

8. Suspend an old single bed metal frame or even an old ladder from the ceiling to give you space to hook your hangers when removing clothes from the drier.

9. Wash soft toys in your machine by putting them in lingerie bags. Remember to check that the eyes and other parts are still secure after washing. Note: this works for plastic toys like Lego as well.

10. If you are spending a lot of time in the laundry, invest in a portable music player or radio to give yourself something to listen to other than the washer and drier.

11. We all appreciate nice and crisp clothes that can give us a professional look. However, most of us hate the ironing required in order to achieve that polished look. You don't have to worry. Here are some tricks that can help you get the job done faster and more efficiently.

12. For the first trick, all you need is aluminum foil. First, remove the ironing protective board cover. Then, simply place a strip of foil on top of the table, and put the protector back on. Because of the heat reflection, you'll be able to smooth out both sides of the clothing at once. This trick does wonders for fabrics like silk, wool, and rayon. If you are traveling, take note that you can use hair straighteners to iron the collar of your polo shirts.

13. Odor in clothes can make you feel like you are wearing something unclean. Food, cigarette smoke, and sweat can stick to your shirt, making you feel like you are untidy. Here are some tricks that you can use to ensure that your clothes are odor-free.

14. Those who go to the gym know how difficult it is to get rid of the stink of sweat and body odor. To make things easier for you, simply rinse the clothing at the gym itself to get rid of the sweat and odor as soon as possible. You can then wash them as usual once you get home. If the odor is strong, simply spray white vinegar on the underarm area before throwing it to the laundry. Vinegar is one of the most

powerful solutions you can use to combat odor. This is guaranteed to keep your clothes smelling clean.

15. If you want to get rid of odor in shoes, the best way to do so is to simply stuff them with socks or with a teabag. They will absorb the unwanted odor that you want to get rid of.

16. Clothes require a lot of care and maintenance. You must exert extra effort if you want to keep your clothes presentable. Here are some tips that you can use to keep your clothes neat-looking.

17. If you get an unexpected ink stain on your clothes, simply rub it off with hand sanitizer and follow up with regular washing later on. If gum accidentally sticks to your child's shirt, stuff the shirt in a plastic bag and put it in your freezer. It will be very easy to remove gum when it is in solid form. If you want to keep buttons in place, simply coat them with clear nail polish so that they won't fall off.

LIFE HACKS FOR YOUR BEDROOM

Your bedroom should be the most comfortable place in your home. It should allow you to relax and feel good about yourself after a long day's work. It should be a place that you would be excited to stay in. It should be clean and organized so that it will be easier for you to rest and sleep. Just because visitors don't usually get to see bedrooms, it does not mean that it should look like it's been hit by a typhoon.

Looking for ways to tidy up your bedroom? Here are some tips that could help you tidy up your bedroom in an efficient manner.

A bedroom is a sanctuary and should be a private retreat for the individual, couple, or kids. Bedrooms are not only for sleeping though. Kids might use their bedrooms for studying or entertain visiting friends, you and your spouse might want to eat breakfast in the bedroom on a Sunday, or you might want to have a quiet spot in the house to read. Whatever the use, it should be a comfortable, stress-free space for every person.

Some quick hacks to optimize your bedroom:
1. There should be no clutter in this room at all. Never use a bedroom as a storage space and get rid of anything that does not belong here.

2. Lighter colors on the walls, furniture, curtains and linen will make the space look bigger.

3. If you want a bright or bold color, accent one wall and match your linen and décor to the wall color. A riot of color is distracting and does not lend itself to tranquility.

4. Use the walls, where ever possible, for storage. Wall-mount the dressing table. A floating dressing table clears some floor space. Use an ottoman with storage space instead of a chair at the dressing table.

5. Design your dressing table around your appliances and needs. Mount a power station (multi-plug) in a drawer to hide loose wires for the hairdryer, curling tongs, rechargeable shavers etc.

6. If storage is a problem, get rid of your side tables and build low or medium chests-of-drawers. These are perfect for jewelry, underwear, tank-tops, shorts and T-shirts. Roll or fold the clothes to be visible from the top. You will save a lot of time by finding your clothes a lot quicker. Stacked clothing in a cupboard inevitably falls over and you waste a lot of space between the top of the stacks and the next shelf.

7. Be creative if you want side tables next to the bed – use a stack of books (with a tray in top), chairs (either standing on the floor or hangings from the wall), baskets, roman columns, drinks trolleys, a bass drum (lying flat, and bonus points for converting the hi-hat into a lamp), trunks and even a slim bookcase can serve as a side table.

8. Use blinds instead of curtains for a modern look. Round off the window with crown molding in a box shape.

9. Light in the bedroom is critical. Make sure that you have ample light for the dressing table as well as a reading corner if you want one. Side lamps for the bed helps with reading as well as when you need to get up in the middle of the night. Make sure you choose the correct lamps for fit in with your décor as well as for their ultimate purpose.

10. Corners in a bedroom are a perfect place for a hanging lamp, hanging plants or just a thick dowel suspended on cables to hang your clothes for the next day. In winter, add a couple of dowels to hang your scarves and hats as an easy reach solution.

11. Make sure that you utilize the space under the bed for storing clothes or shoes that are out of season.

12. If you are in the market for a new bed, purchase one with storage space in the base of the bed.

13. To optimize the storage of clothes, place them in sturdy bags and use your vacuum cleaner to suck out the air. Seal the bag, and it will take up a fraction of the space and keep the clothes free from mold, insects and smells. Note: Zip-lock bags for this purpose are available in stores as well as online and they have handy vacuum seals built into the sides. Use them in your suitcase as well to pack double the volume of clothes when travelling.

14. Use pool noodles or hollow core cardboard tubes in your boots to keep them upright and neat.

15. In most bedrooms, space is often a problem. More often than not, we have too many things so everything just looks like a cluttered mess. There are bedrooms with too much furniture too. This could make it difficult for you to move around.

16. When you have to organize your room, you have to think of ways to maximize space. More often than not, rooms can be easily organized simply by re-arranging furniture and maximizing open space.

17. You will be surprised by how much you can maximize space. For example, the walls are never just for pictures and posters. You can simply hang hooks on walls and then use it to store your bags, purses, scarves, and other accessories.

18. Don't ignore the space behind doors too. You can hang stuff behind your doors. It is ideal for storing things that you pick up just before leaving your home.

19. We know how difficult it is to have clothes for different seasons. As you rotate clothing, you must know how to maximize space to store the ones that are not in use. You can store unused clothes under the bed to maximize space. Just bring them out when it is time to use them again.

20. Use chair pockets to help you organize your things. This is ideal for storing stationary supplies and other things that you often use. You can hook your chair pocket to your wall for easy access.

21. You must learn how to maximize your closets too. You'll be surprised to know that simply adding shelves in your closet will maximize space. You can easily DIY shelves if you purchase the correct materials. Ask your local hardware store about what can help you install shelves in cabinets and closets.

22. Your bedroom furniture makes a huge difference in the way your bedroom looks. From the moment you purchase your furniture, try to make sure that you have efficiency in mind. Go for dual-purpose furniture. For example, choose a mirror that doubles as storage space. Choose a chair that can also be used as a bed in case you have sudden guests who need to sleepover.

23. When you arrange your furniture, try to angle them at the corner of the room. For example, angling a couch on the corner will allow you to have some space behind which will allow you to store stuff like CDs or umbrellas.

LIFE HACKS FOR YOUR BATHROOM

Maintaining a clean and functional bathroom is important for your family's hygiene. You don' have to invest in expensive bathroom products just for bathroom maintenance. Here are some of the things you can do to help improve your bathroom.

• When in a bathroom, try to maximize space too. You can do this by being innovative in storing your things. You can use various household items for efficient storage.

• You can use a spice rack for placing your bottled toiletries like hair products and lotions. For a shared bathroom, use coat hooks for storing towels in use. For extra towels, roll them up when you store them because they take up less space. It will also make your bathroom feel like a spa.

• Use small storage solutions to easily find your stuff. Keep big containers under the sink and re-fill bottles as needed. Use a magnet strip to line up your Bobby pins or hair clips on your mirror.

• Choose a large mirror for your bathroom. It is very useful because it will allow you to see your whole self when dressing up. Aside from this, you will also feel like your bathroom is bigger because a mirror creates the illusion of depth.

Life hacks for Your Lawn & Garden

Your front lawn is what people see when they look at your house. You must exert efforts to make your lawn look neat in order to leave the right impression with your guests and visitors. In addition to this, lawns are often spacious. You will easily be able to maximize your lawns if you know life hacks and tricks that can help you.

The most simple life hack you can do is turning an old milk jug into a watering can, simply by puncturing holes in the cap. For an impromptu shade during the summertime, you can use an ordinary curtain to help protect your plants. Attach one end of your house and the other one on a pole or tree, and simply slide across as needed.

Cleaning garden tools can be very difficult. For removing dust and soil from any of your garden tools, take pieces of crumpled aluminum foil and dip it in water. Use the aluminum to scrub away the things that you don't want. In case your tools look old and rusty, you can use white vinegar to help break down the rust.

Life hacks for Your Garage

Do not make the mistake of ignoring your garage. The garage is full of hazards, so it is important to store your things efficiently in order to keep the area safe. You must also do what you can to ensure that your garage is safe. It contains quite a lot of expensive tools and it probably serves as storage space for your car as well. You have to make sure that you keep bad people away from your garage in order to ensure the safety of your family and your property.

The most basic practice that you can do to keep your garage clean is to avoid storing everything in there. Go ahead and throw the non-essentials.

Here are some other life hacks which can help you maximize space, and at the same time help keep your garage accident-free.

• Simple curtains can do wonders in making your garage look a bit homey. No matter how much you organize your tools into baskets or shelves, they will never look aesthetically pleasing. For aesthetic purposes, hang curtains in front of your storage area. Simply slide the curtains, and you will instantly be able to use the other half of your garage any way you want.

• To store your things in the garage, it is a good idea to build a vertical shelf where you can store your tools, sporting goods, and other materials. Shelves are pretty easy to build. Get your supplies in a hardware store, and start building your shelf now!

• One thing that you should watch out for is how you park your car in your garage. Use pool noodles to cushion the walls against accidental bumps in your car. Cut and drill pool noodles onto the walls of your garage to cushion those blows to your car doors. This will allow you to save a ton of money on paint jobs. In case your car already has scratches, use nail polish to cover up the scratch.

• Your garage contains a lot of valuable items which could attract burglars around your area. Make sure that you safeguard your garage because, aside from containing expensive tools and gadgets like your car, it is also the entrance to your home. Install a motion sensor light; a floodlight that detects motion is ideal. Install the light high enough that it's not easy to smash or dismantle

Clearing up more Space around the House

Do you feel like you have too much stuff? Are you bothered because your house seems so small because you have too many possessions?

Very few homeowners actually pay attention to space management. They always think that they need to have a bigger home in order to have more space. In reality, only proper space management is necessary in order to make the space more functional. Your home can accommodate more things if you know how to store them properly.

For example, you may use a tension rod in your sink cabinet to create a horizontal bar for hanging your spray bottle cleaners. Imagine all the floor space you will save!

There are many other tricks that you can use! Just be creative in using the things around you. For example, tissue boxes and cardboard tubes are perfect for storing plastic grocery bags neatly. Look around your home! What are the items that you can adjust?

CLEANING HACKS

Before I discovered cleaning hacks, whenever I encountered a stain that was hard to remove, I just accepted it as damaged and unable to be cleaned. A few years ago my two sons picked up permanent markers from a kitchen drawer and decided that our newly painted kitchen wall would be a great place to draw a mural. I desperately tried to clean the marker off using multiple cleaning agents and wasn't able to get the marks off.

Then I started to do some digging because surely someone else had run into this problem and found a way to clean their wall. By the time I was done researching, I knew how to get permanent marker off of virtually any surface! Let's take a look at some clever, creative cleaning hacks that will make cleaning super easy.

1. Get Stains Out of Microfiber. Getting stains on microfiber can ruin the entire look of your sofa. If you have a spill or stain on the fabric, fill a spray bottle with rubbing alcohol and lightly mist the alcohol onto the stain. Gently rub the moistened stain with a white soft sponge. The stain will lift right onto the sponge. Let the sofa air dry completely. Once dry, take a hard bristled brush to "fluff" up the microfibers and your sofa will look like new.

2. Remove Permanent Marker Stains. Permanent marker stains don't have to be permanent! Hand sanitizer will remove marker stains from clothing. If you get marker on any wood surface, you can easily remove it by applying rubbing alcohol to the affected area. Applying toothpaste or hairspray to marks on walls will eliminate the stain.

3. If you get marker on your carpet, dab the area with white vinegar and the stain will be removed. If you spill marker onto furniture, take a cotton ball and dip it into milk. Applying directly to the stain will remove the mark.

4. Prevent Dust Bunnies When Dusting Your Ceiling Fan. I used to dread cleaning my ceiling fans because getting dust all over the carpet or bed was inevitable. Then I discovered a way to contain the dust bunnies. Take an old, soft pillowcase and insert each fan blade into the pillowcase. Wipe each blade of the inner part of the fan to the outer part. All the dust will stay contained in the bottom of the pillowcase.

5. Easily Clean Your Electric Oven. Years ago, cleaning your oven was a hassle. You either used harsh chemicals to get the gunk off or had to scrub the caked on layers of filth incessantly to get it clean. I found a much easier way. You will want to make sure you start this process with a cold oven.

6. Take a shallow dish and pour ½ cup of ammonia into it. Place the dish in the middle of the top rack in your oven. Close the door and let it sit in there overnight. The fumes from the ammonia will loosen the grit. In the morning, take a clean cloth and wipe it all away. Only use this method in an electric oven.

7. Clean You're Charcoal Grill Naturally. As crazy as it sounds, the most effective way to clean your charcoal grill is to use an onion. Yes, an onion. This is a natural way where you don't have to worry about any harsh chemical residue being left to creep into your grilled food. Here's how it works.

8. Heat your grill so the high heat burns off any remaining chunks of charred food. Peel an onion and slice it in half. Insert a fork into the bottom part of the onion, towards the round part. Turn the heat down. Rub the onion flat side down onto the grill, moving it quickly back and forth. This will clean and deglaze the grates, not to mention adding an amazing flavor to your next meal.

9. Eradicate Oil Stains from Your Garage Floor. This trick is super easy, effective and a bit disturbing. Pour Coca-Cola directly onto the oil stain and rub with a hard bristled brush. Rinse off thoroughly with clean water. Watch as the stain lifts from the floor.

10. Get Rid of Lipstick Stains. It's rare that you can get a noticeable lipstick stain out of clothing from just washing your clothes normally. The next time you encounter a stain, spray some hairspray onto the mark and let it sit for 10 minutes. Rub gently with a cloth and toss into the wash as normal.

11. Eliminate Kitchen Cabinet Gunk. Over time our kitchen cabinets get dirty, often times with tiny little particles of dust, debris and food from splashing when cooking. And it piles on resulting in a solid substance that is near impossible to remove. Here's an easy way you can lift the stains so your cabinets look brand new.

12. Create a thick paste by combing vegetable oil and baking soda so the consistency is like toothpaste. Take an old toothbrush and scrub the nooks and crannies on your cabinets where the debris has piled up. Take a moist, clean cloth and remove the paste and debris.

13. A muffin tin can be used to serve the condiments at barbecues and parties. In addition to looking good, it helps you cut down on washing. Think twice before discarding your muffin tins next time.

14. You can easily pull out the egg shells from the egg in a bowl if you wet your fingers.

15. You can remove the stem of an avocado to see how ripe it is. If it appears yellowish, it is ripe; if it appears dark brown, it is overripe.

16. To make bananas last about 5 days longer, wrap their tops tightly in a plastic wrap.

17. Pour milk in an ice cube tray and add crushed cookies (or Oreos) in it to make cookie ice cubes.

18. Unscented dental floss can be used to easily cut or slice cakes, pastries, and other soft solid goods into perfect shapes.

18. Unscented dental floss can be used to easily cut or slice cakes, pastries, and other soft solid goods into perfect shapes.

19. Give more shape and designs to your pancakes by using cookie cutters.

20. When storing salad in a sealed bag, blow some air into it to ensure that it stays fresh longer.

21. When going grocery shopping, open your fridge and take a picture. Look at it before you leave the shop to make sure that you have not forgotten anything.

22. You can freeze grapes and use them to chill white wine. Unlike ice, the grapes will not water it down.

23. To keep ice-cream soft, put it in an airtight bag before storing it in the freezer. It won't be spoon-bendingly hard when you take it out.

24. To prevent the pizza crust from getting chewy when microwaving it, put a glass of water along with it in the microwave when reheating it.

25. To keep the potatoes from budding, place an apple among them when storing them.

26. When cutting an onion, if you chew a chewing gum, your eyes will not burn or water.

27. To make sure that your cake stays soft and moist, put a slice of bread over it.

28. When boiling something, put a wooden spoon or stick over it to keep it from spilling.

29. When storing meat in plastic bags, section it evenly. It makes it easier to remove even sized pieces later.

30. If you wrap lettuce, celery, or broccoli in a foil when storing it in the fridge, it will stay crisp longer than usual.

31. To test the freshness of an egg, put it in a glass filled with water. If it floats, it is not fresh, throw it away. If it sinks to the bottom, it is fresh.

32. Instead of letting a sauce go to waste, put it in an ice cube tray and freeze it. Remove a cube and heat it when needed.

33. To easily peel garlic, smash it apart by applying pressure from the top. Then put it all inside a box and shake it. When you remove it, the garlic will be peeled.

34. When reheating food, like pasta, spread it evenly on a plate and create an opening in the center, giving it a doughnut shape. It will allow the food to be re-heated properly and from all sides.

35. To make the onions last very long, put them in a pantyhose and tie knots above each onion. This way, they can last for up to 8 months.

36. Green onions can also last very long if they are frozen. Just be sure that you have dried them completely before storing them.

37. To prevent the cutting board from sliding when cutting vegetables, place a damp towel under it.

38. You can use a pizza cutter to cut pancakes too.

39. To extract more juice from a lemon, roll it by applying a little pressure before cutting it.

40. The skin of a ginger can easily be removed with a spoon.

41. When using a measuring cup to measure a liquid, like honey, spray it with non-stick spray first. This way, the liquid will not stick in the cup and your measurements will be more accurate.

42. To restore old crystallized honey, put the jar of honey in warm water for 15 minutes or so.

43. Freezing herbs in olive oil keep them fresh and prevents them from turning brown or getting freezer burns.

44. If you boil filtered water to make ice, the resulting ice will be clear as a crystal.

45. Fish often falls apart or breaks when it is being grilled. Place halved lemon slices on a grill and cook fish over it to make sure that you get it in one piece.

46. Storing ginger in the freezer makes it last longer.

47. Always store mushrooms in a paper bag instead of a plastic bag. The paper bag will absorb all the moisture and keep them from getting mildew.

COOKING

I'm always searching to find new cooking hacks that will make cooking fun and easy. I've compiled some of the most useful hacks I have found over the years below at will make you efficient in the kitchen and execute complex dishes flawlessly.

1. How often when you're standing in the kitchen trying to cook a simple meal for the family, or reheating the leftovers do you have two bowls that both need heating up, yet only 1 ever fits in the microwave. You end up sitting there for 8 long minutes and then have to do the same again. You end up with a hot one and warm or cold one depending on time.

What can you do?
Get your two bowls as normal and place one in the microwave as you normally would. Get a mug and put inside the microwave next to the bowl and place the second bowl on top of the mug.... Problem solved.

2. Think of all those times that you stood in the kitchen cracking your eggs into a bowl to make an omelette for lunch, only for that last horrible egg not to split right and you end up with little bits of shell in your lunch. You can either leave it and crunch on it later or spend half an hour trying to grab it with your fingers only to give up.

What can you do?
If you get one of the empty egg shells and use it to get the small piece of shell out you will find that for some unknown reason the shell is kind of attracted to the bigger shell and comes out right away.... Problem solved.

3. When you wake up in the morning on a hot clammy summer day, but you need your morning coffee. You end up with the choice of having a normal hot coffee,

which isn't very refreshing on a hot day. Or end up diluting you're your coffee with ice cubes.

What can you do?
Try smashing up Oreo and placing the bits in an ice cube tray. Fill it with cold coffee and freeze overnight. When you wake up drop a couple into your iced coffee. YUM... Problem solved.

4. When the kids are out playing and come running in asking for an iced cream. You go in the freezer, take out that giant tub of three flavor iced cream and end up bending your spoons trying to get out a good size scoop for those cones. You either have to wait half an hour for it to soften or replace your spoons every time.

What can you do?
Try getting a large zip lock back and keep your tub of ice cream in it. Next time you take out of the freezer and remove it from the bag you will notice it is always slightly soft. No more bent spoons... Problem solved.

5. You're standing in the kitchen cooking a nice romantic meal for your partner. You're just about to add some nice herbs and you spot that your little bag of herbs has gone bad, and it's a trip to the shop or use those horrid dry herbs you get in a jar.

What can you do?
When you first get your bag of herbs chop, then put them in an ice cube tray and cover with oil then freeze. The oil stops your herbs getting freezer burn and keeps them nice and fresh for when needed... Problem solved.

6. You have a few friends around for a meal. It gets to desert time and you go in the cupboard and you suddenly realize that all you have is mixed up bowls that down match.

What can you do?

Try melting a big bar of chocolate and dipping blown up balloons in. When the chocolate hardens, pop the balloons and you're left with beautiful bowls that go down a treat... Problem solved.

7. When you go into your kitchen and do the washing up. You wipe down the sides and chopping boards. You get your cleaning spray out and clean away. But then the next time you go to make a sandwich it tastes funny because of the spray.

What can you do?

Try using salt and half a lemon. This kills the bacteria and lets you clean your chopping boards and you avoid the chemicals...Problem solved.

8. If you're anything like me, you will have a cupboard filled with random spice jars and nowhere else to keep them apart from dotted around your work tops

What can you do?

Try using an old CD rack. Most people have an old one lying around from the days before mp3 players. If not they are often a lot cheaper than actual spice racks and do the job perfectly... Problem solved.

9. Picture it. It's a hot summer day and you fancy a nice iced lolly. All you have in your freezer are those horrid little ice pops that taste like colored water. You can either go out, or spend load of money on 3 little lollies that are ok or you can suffer with the cheaper ice pops.

What can you do?

Best iced lollies I have ever tasted. Mix together and freeze and an iced lolly mold.

2 cups of whipped cream

1 cup of milk

6 tbsp. Nutella

You will never go back. Yum...Problem solved.

10. I always get tooth ache and when I have a drink, I end up using a straw to help with the pain. It gets kind of embarrassing though when every 2 seconds the straw rises up from your can and pokes you in the face.

What can you do?
Try turning the little metal tab around and put your straw through the hole in the center of the tab. It stops you getting poked in the eye and you avoid the tooth-ache... Problem solved.

11. Let's face it, on a roasting hot day when you're out during the off day, the worst thing is carrying a lukewarm bottle of water around with you. We don't always have the money to go into shops to keep buying nice cold ones.

What can you do?
Try filling a large bottle quarter of the way up and laying it down flat in your freezer. Next time your off out, fill it up and will stay cold on your trip out... Problem solved.

12. So it's breakfast time and there's a decision to be made. Half the people you're cooking for want bacon and the other half want pancakes.

What can you do?
Try cooking your bacon in the frying pan. When done pour over a little pancake mix and cook as normal. You're now the proud maker of the bacon pancake. Pour over some syrup. Yum... Problem solved.

13. How many times have you stood there in your kitchen holding that cookbook and the dreaded words separate the egg yolks appear. You end up getting horrible slimy fingers or end up not bothering and just going with the whole egg.

What can you do?
Try cracking your egg as normal into a bowl. Get a clean, empty bottle and place

the top over the yolk and squeeze. The yolk will get sucked up into the end of the bottle ready to pop back where you need. No more slimy fingers... Problem solved.

14. You wake up in the middle of the night with the sudden urge for a spot of cake. Or the kids have just had tea and want some desert but you have none in and no time to bake one.

What can you do?
A brownie in less than 2 minutes? Sounds like a plan.
Mix together in a cup until smooth, and then cook in the microwave for 1 minute 40 seconds. Yum.
¼ cup sugar
¼ cup flour
2 tbsp cocoa
Pinch salt
2 tbsp olive oil
3 tbsp water
Problem solved.

15. When you're standing in the kitchen trying to look all manly while cooking some dinner. You get to the onions and stand there with tears streaming down your face like a baby.

What can you do?
Chew gum while chopping onions it stops you from crying... Problem solved.

16. Whenever I use a block of cheese or have a large cake, I go digging through the draw routing around for a knife I can use to get nice neat slices. The trouble is, the only thing I can ever find is the standard blunt butter knife.

What can you do?

Try using an unscented dental floss. It works a treat and a pack lasts ages. You can use it to slice up pretty much anything that isn't too hard... Problem solved.

17. Do you miss being able to make a decent toasted sandwich because all you currently have is the standard two slice toaster. The only thing you can think of is to toast two slices of bread, stick on some kind of filler and slap them both together.

What can you do?

Try making a sandwich as normal squashing the bread together and put the whole sandwich into one toaster slot. The result is a nice toasted sandwich that is still soft in the middle. Yum... Problem solved.

18. I find it so annoying when you go out to the supermarket and you spend an hour picking up everything you need. You get to the till pack up and go home. As soon as you finish putting all your stuff away you realize that you have forgotten a few important things. You can either go back or go without.

What can you do?

Try taking a photo of the inside of your fridge so while you're out shopping you can see what you have and what you don't... Problem solved.

19. We all do it, don't we? We go out and buy a load of fresh fruit and veg and but the time we get round to actually eat them, half have gone bad. Bananas seem to be the worst.

What can you do?

Try wrapping some plastic wrap around the stem of the bananas and you will notice that this keeps them fresher for longer... Problem solved.

20. I love a nice takeaway. You order a giant pizza for the family; there are a few pieces left in the morning and naturally you stick it in the microwave and reheat it

for breakfast. When you take it out the crust is either rock solid or really chewy.

What can you do?
Try placing a glass of water in the microwave next to the pizza. The steam helps it stay soft but stops it going all chewy... Problem solved.

21. I find it so irritating when you reheat food in the microwave and it's steamy and feels hot, yet when you sit down to eat it half of it in the middle is still cold. You end up carrying on and pay for it the next day or pay another trip to the kitchen for round two. This usually results in dry burn food that goes in the bin.

What can you do?
Dig a hole in the middle of the food so you can see the plate. Now when it goes in the microwave it will heat nice an evenly... Problem solved.

22. My kids love spaghetti and hotdogs, but sometimes and can get a little boring for them.

What can you do?
Try this little tip. Get the kids to help too. Chop up your hotdogs into quarters and pierce a few pieces of dry spaghetti through the middle and boil as normal. Mix in a little ketchup when done and sprinkle with cheese. The kids will love it... Problem solved.

23. I always take a packed lunch to work but I like something different now and then so I'll take a bagel. The problem is the filling always falls out. You end up with a bald bagel and bag of sandwich filler.

What can you do?
We all have those old CD spindles lying around. Give a clean out and it makes a great bagel holder. Yum... Problem solved.

24. Many of us out there turn into a bit of a clean freak now and then. I myself have been getting dirty hands, but I love nothing more than milk and Oreos. Problem is I hate getting all the mess on my fingers.

What can you do?
Use a fork in the middle of the Oreo. You get your treat with none of the miss... Problem solved.

25. Do you ever pick up a pizza on the way from work only to find that it's gone cold by the time you arrive home?

What can you do?
Try using your seat warmer. Most people don't think of it but it works a treat... Problem solved.

26. Do you remember that time you had the girls round for a movie, chat and a bottle of wine only to find that the corkscrew has gone missing. You end up spending half an hour trying to get the cork out and come to the solution that the only thing to do is push it in instead.

What can you do?
Try using a hammer and nail. Gently hammer the nail into the cork and then use the claw to pull it and the cork back out... Problem solved.

27. I think we have all ruined a few cook books haven't we. We get a nice one for a Christmas and give it a whirl. Next minute you notice you have a grease of food marks all over the pages or something has splashed on the side and got the pages all wet.

What can you do?
Find and pants hanger with the clip on each side. It works great to hold a book and hang where you can use it... Problem solved.

28. I love tacos. The problem is when you cook the shell and can't get it the right shape. It's either a flat circle or you fold it and it falls on its self. No good.

What can you do?
Try using a muffin tin. Turn it upside down and put your taco shells in the spaces. Spray with oil and cook at 375F for 10 minutes. Perfect... Problem solved.

29. You wake up in the morning, go in the kitchen and boil a couple of eggs. You fancy some sliced egg or egg mayo with lunch but it takes forever to peel the shell of the egg.

What can you do?
Add a teaspoon of baking soda into the water before you start boiling your eggs. Now when it comes to peeling the shells off it will just seconds... Problem solved.

30. A random thought. How do you eat a cupcake? If it's a large one with butter cream all over the top you end up with quite a sickly taste after a while.

What can you do?
This is the right way to eat a cupcake. Slice it through the middle and place the bottom half of the cake into the top, to make a kind of which sandwich. You will never eat a cupcake the same way again... Problem solved.

31. The thing that bugs me when I make pasta or boil potatoes is when the water boils over and leaves you with a big messy clean up job.

What can you do?
If you place a wooden spoon on the top of the pan as the water boils it stops the water ever boiling over... Problem solved.

32. My kids love pancakes but it can be a bit of a pain making up the mixture every day and getting splatters over your side. You can either put the horrid readymade

stuff or persist and clean up each time.

What can you do?
Try pouring your pancake mix into an empty large ketchup bottle. It will keep in the fridge and save all the mess than if you used a bowl and ladle... Problem solved.

33. It's summer time and you have the family round for a BBQ. Everyone wants a different sauce and it's a real pain trying to find somewhere for all those dips and bottles.

What can you do?
Use a muffin tin. Pour some of each condiment into the tin and leave by the BBQ. Now everyone has what they want on hand... Problem solved.

34. Have you ever tried to remove the stem from a strawberry when making a desert? You either end up using a knife and wasting half of the fruit, or leaving it in there as a crunchy woody surprise.

What can you do?
Use a straw place it over the top of the stem and push down. Stem removed... Problem solved.

35. It's horrible when you wake up late for work. You rush to get ready and make a coffee. Just before you leave your coffee is still roasting and you have the choice to leave it and miss your caffeine fix, or water it down with a little cold water. Either way, your morning is ruined.

What can you do?
Try keeping some frozen black coffee in some ice cube trays. This way, if you're ever in this situation again, you can cool down your coffee without watering it down... Problem solved.

36. You and your partner have just put the kids to bed for a nice warm day. You settle down to have a glass of white wine only to discover you forgot to put it in the fridge. You can either water it down with an ice cube or take it warm.

What can you do?
Keep a bag of grapes in the freezer. No need to water that wine down. The grapes do a great job of cooling it... Problem solved.

Last little food hack.
When you're down to the last bit of Nutella in the jar. Don't sit scraping away stick a dollop of ice cream in. Lovely little treat.

37. Prep Potatoes for a Crowd Easily. I'm well known for making potato dishes around the holidays or for special events that will feed a huge crowd. Instead of standing over my kitchen sink scrubbing 10 pounds of potatoes, I rinse them off in my dishwasher. Here's how you do it.

Place your potatoes on the top rack only and turn the setting to the rinse cycle. Don't add any detergent and be sure to set the drying setting to "air dry". This is a super effective way to get your potatoes clean quickly. You can also rinse off other root vegetables this way.

38. Create Clean Cuts. The best way to create clean cuts on soft or crumbly food is to use unflavored dental floss. You can cut clean, precise slices of cakes and brownies. You can slice a sheet of cake horizontally to create an extra layer in your cake. I've used floss to cut through cookie dough to make uniform pieces, as well as soft cheeses.

You can create perfect, straight slices when using it to cut through a log-shaped cookies, as well as cinnamon rolls. If you don't have butcher's twine when cooking a roast, you can substitute it with dental floss in a pinch.

39. Make and Preserve Guacamole. If you don't have a fancy mortar and pestle to smash avocados when making guacamole, you can still make an amazing guacamole. Carve out the flesh of the avocados and place them into a bowl. To get perfect avocado chunks for your guacamole, simply mash the avocado flesh with a hand held potato masher.

Once you have made your guacamole and you want to save it for the next day, add it to a bowl that only has an inch or two of space between the top of the guacamole and top of the bowl. Slowly add some water to the top and cover with plastic wrap. The water won't seep into the guac, but will prevent it from browning. When you are ready to eat it, simply dump out the water on top and enjoy.

40. Remove Fat From Stews, Soups and Casseroles. Take a couple of ice cubes and drop it into your stew, soup or casserole dish. Fat globules will start to solidify on the top from the colder temperature. Scoop out the extra fat and save on fat and calories.

41. Take the Bread out of Bread Crumbs. If you are trying to eat gluten free, you can still enjoy "breaded" chicken. Take some gluten free pretzels or some brown rice cereal, and place them in a food processor. Hit the pulse button until the pretzels or cereal has a breadcrumb-like consistency. Shake and bake as normal, or coat the chicken with milk and egg, then add the crumb mixture and bake.

42. Prevent Bacon Shrinkage. Ah, bacon! Yummy, delicious bacon! Whether you cook bacon in the oven, stove top or microwave, you always end up with some shrinkage. You can reduce shrinkage by up to 50% by rinsing the bacon off with cold water before cooking it.

43. Cook Crispy, Bright, Flavorful Vegetables in Your Oven. Say goodbye to dull, mushy vegetables that have completely lost their flavor. Take any soft veggie, like asparagus, green beans or pea pods and cook them inside a head of lettuce. This method has actually been used for years to create crispier, more vibrant vegetables in the oven.

Slice a head of iceberg lettuce down the center. Scoop out the leaves inside, so the halves retain its shape, but have a little pod for the veggies. Add the veggies, put the head of lettuce back together again with the veggies inside and roast on a cookie sheet on 300F for 20 – 45 minutes.

44. Avoid Clumps in Brown Sugar. The best way to keep brown sugar in your pantry from becoming hard and clumpy is to store it in an airtight container once it has been opened. Then add a couple of marshmallows to the container to prevent any hardening or clumps.

A muffin tin can be used to serve the condiments at barbecues and parties. In addition to looking good, it helps you cut down on washing. Think twice before discarding your muffin tins next time.

45. You can easily pull out the egg shells from the egg in a bowl if you wet your fingers.

46. You can remove the stem of an avocado to see how ripe it is. If it appears yellowish, it is ripe; if it appears dark brown, it is overripe.

47. To make bananas last about 5 days longer, wrap their tops tightly in a plastic wrap.

48. Pour milk in an ice cube tray and add crushed cookies (or Oreos) in it to make cookie ice cubes.

49. Unscented dental floss can be used to easily cut or slice cakes, pastries, and other soft solid goods into perfect shapes.

50. Give more shape and designs to your pancakes by using cookie cutters.

51. When storing salad into a sealed bag, blow some air into it to ensure that it stays fresh longer.

52. When going grocery shopping, open your fridge and take a picture. Look at it before you leave the shop to make sure that you have not forgotten anything.

53. You can freeze grapes and use them to chill white wine. Unlike ice, the grapes will not water it down.

54. To keep ice-cream soft, put it in an airtight bag before storing it in the freezer. It won't be spoon-bendingly hard when you take it out.

55. To prevent the pizza crust from getting chewy when microwaving it, put a glass of water along with it in the microwave when reheating it.

56. To keep the potatoes from budding, place an apple among them when storing them.

57. When cutting an onion, if you chew a chewing gum, your eyes will not burn or water.

58. To make sure that your cake stays soft and moist, put a slice of bread over it.

59. When boiling something, put a wooden spoon or stick over it to keep it from spilling.

60. When storing meat in plastic bags, section it evenly. It makes it easier to remove even sized pieces later.

61. If you wrap lettuce, celery, or broccoli in a foil when storing it in the fridge, it will stay crisp longer than usual.

62. To test the freshness of an egg, put it in a glass filled with water. If it floats, it is not fresh, throw it away. If it sinks to the bottom, it is fresh.

63. Instead of letting a sauce go to waste, put it in an ice cube tray and freeze it. Remove a cube and heat it when needed.

64. To easily peel garlic, smash it apart by applying pressure from the top. Then put it all inside a box and shake it. When you remove it, the garlic will be peeled.

TOP TIPS.

Keeping you and your home cool in those hot clammy months.

• Try not to exercise just before going to bed. When you exercise it raises your body temperature and your body will retain heat. Instead exercise a couple of hours before.

• Take a tepid shower or bath. If you try taking a cold your body can react by trying to heat up which is the opposite of what you want.

• Heat rises so if you struggle to sleep at night, try putting your mattress on the floor or sleep on a lower level of the house.

• Before bed, try putting your sheets and pillows in the freezer they should stay cool enough for you to fall asleep nice and comfortable.

• When to hot sleep in cotton not nude. Cotton allows your body to breath and lets moisture evaporate between you and your sheets.

• Run cold water over your wrists for about 30 seconds. Your wrist is where blood flows closest to the surface of your body. This cools your blood and cools your whole body.

MONEY HACKS

Everyone wants to save money. They want to have enough left over at the end of the month so that they are able to put a little away. You might want to do it for some security, for your retirement, to put some towards a trip, or for many other reasons. But it can get really easy to spend the money that you have on things that aren't important or that you just do not need and soon all of your money is gone. Here are some great tips to follow when you are ready to start saving money today.

Spend Less.

The best way to make sure that you are saving money is to spend less of it. This means that you need to find ways to cut out your spending, whether this means shopping less, eating out less, or finding ways to cut down on your bills. To start with are the extra expenses; you do not need to go out and purchase expensive shoes all of the time or go out with your friends several times a week. Stay home, rent a few cheap movies, and make supper most nights and you will be amazed at how much you can save. In addition, look through your bills and see where you might be able to cut corners. Limit the amount of channels that you have (who needs 200?) and call your cable or your phone company and see if they will give you discounts for being a loyal customer. These things may be little but they will save you a lot of money in the long run.

Budget

One thing that most people fail to do is create a budget. They feel that they do not need it or do not want to put in the work that is required for it. But a budget is a great tool if you want to make sure that all of your money is going to the right place. After creating one, you might be surprised at the areas where you are spending a lot of money and can then cut back without feeling the pinch as much. Once you create a budget, make sure that you stick with it for the long term and try not to go for it.

Buy Used

You can save a ton of money if you just learn how to purchase used things instead of new. While buying used has a stigma around it because used means old, it is time to get over that because you can find many great things for a fraction of the cost. Instead of spending $100 on a pair of jeans, you could purchase a whole wardrobe, along with some shoes and matching jewelry for about that much. Check out garage sales, online sites, and your local thrift shops for the best deals.

Get Rid of Debt

The debt that you have is often going to cost you more than it is worth. This is due to the fact that you are going to have to pay interest on it and that can add up quickly. A few dollars on a credit card or a loan is quickly going to add up and cause you a headache. Pay down your debt as quickly as possible and find ways that you will be able to avoid debt in the future. Just losing the interest payments on the money you owe will put so much more back into your pockets.

Shop Smartly

To save money you have to learn how to be a smart shopper. You cannot be taken in by the big sale signs or tricked into purchasing things that are not a good deal. Learn where the best deals are, avoid shopping if it is your weakness, and learn how to not purchase things that you do not need, even if they are on sale.

Eat In

You would be amazed at the amount of money that you might spend on eating out. Even just doing it once or twice a week can quickly add up and cost you a lot. To really save money, cut out the amount of times that you eat out and instead choose to make meals at home. You can easily feed your family several meals or more on the amount you spend at restaurants and you can put this money in savings or to pay off your debts. Of course it is fine to eat out on occasion, just try to save these for when they are special occasions.

In this declining economy, nothing is more important than managing money. Whether you are doing well financially or barely making ends meet, it is important to keep the flow of money in control. The difficult times can knock anyone off their feet, but if you manage your money properly, you won't have much to worry about. Following are another some life hacks for managing money:

1. Make a box to save your $1 bills. At the end of each day, throw in all the cents, pennies, and $1 bills in it. Even if you throw in $3 each day, by the end of the year you will have $1095 saved.

2. When you get a discount, buy something for sale, get something from a clearance sale at 50% off, instead of wasting the saved money on something else, put it in your savings to actually save it.

3. When you go shopping, try to buy items in bulk. You can save more by bulk buying than you can by purchasing each item individually.

4. When booking tickets online, use 'private browsing' or 'incognito' mode. Many websites show higher rates to returning customers.

5. Use a money management app to manage and plan your finances, and to keep a record of your expenditures. Such apps are available for smart phones, windows, OS X, etc.

6. When getting change from a shop, go for $50 or $100 bills. Research suggests that we are less likely to break $50 and $100 bills.

7. Buy gift cards at discounted prices during holiday seasons, and use them later for shopping to save money.

8. The amenities you use often rack up high bills. Find how much each amenity costs you, and optimize your use to lower the bills.

9. Sell your used electronics and gadgets on the secondary market when you no longer need them. The better condition they are in, the more you can sell them for.

10. Save up on the bills by unplugging the electronics that you are not using. For instance, a microwave uses electricity when it flashes the time all the time, even when it is not being used.

11. You can save a lot on your bills by adjusting the thermostat. Adjust the temperature of the central heating and water heating, so it does the job properly, but do not turn it to very high. Experiment with the temperatures to find the suitable one.

12. Follow this simple rule: spend less than what you earn.

13. Invest in renewable energy. Install a solar plant for generating electricity and save money on the electricity bills. If you generate more energy than you need, the power supplying company will buy it from you, and will either give you the money or subtract the extra from your bills.

14. When buying books for a new college or university term, sell the old ones first, and then buy used copies of the books you need. You can save 25% to 50% of the original book cost by buying a used one instead.

TIPS TO SAVE YOU TIME

There are just so many things that you have to do during the day, it is easy to get behind and wonder how you will ever catch up. This is a dilemma that many Americans face as they try to fit a week's worth of work into just a few hours. If you feel like you are always behind without a way to get caught up, follow some of the suggestions in this chapter to get back on track.

Be Organized

You will be amazed at how much time you have been wasting on finding things that are needed just to get started. You might have misplaced your notes or set the pen down in the wrong spot. Finding keys is difficult and your coat seems to have disappeared. These are all things that are cutting into your productivity and will waste a lot of time. Rather than spending so much of your life trying to find things, you need to learn how to be organized. Find a place for all of your things and then take care that you put them there every time you are done using them. This can help you get to work faster and saves a ton of time.

No Multitasking

Most people feel that multitasking is the way to get more done, but this is a huge time waster. It has been shown that multitasking is going to reduce your productivity by about 40%. This is thought to be due to the fact that going from one task to another is going to make it difficult to get rid of distractions as well as this skipping around will cause blocks in your mental capacity. This combines to slow down the process that you need.

Have a Calendar

It is easy to forget about the things that you need to get done during the day and soon you might find that more than one thing is at the same time or you have more work than you can handle because you forgot about another task. To avoid this and to keep yourself on track, get a calendar and write everything down. Write down projects, due dates, appointments, meetings, nights out, vacations, and any-thing else that is important to your schedule. Make sure that you only have one calendar though. Some people will have multiple ones and this is bound to lead to trouble. Having all the information in one place makes it easier ot know what you need to do and to plan ahead.

Plan Trips and Chores

You can waste a lot of time going back and forth to the store or going around town to do chores. Before going out to run errands, take a few minutes to plan your route and to write a list. Pick the route that makes the most sense and know exactly how to get there without distractions. With the list, you are sure to grab everything that you need and you will not have to waste your time going back out and getting the stuff again.

Routines

Having a routine is the best way to save time. With a routine, you will know when something is going to happen and how much time you have to get it done. The routine might not make you work more productively, but it can help you to know what is coming, where things are, and how to get things done. Another benefit is that a routine is able to free up your brain to do other things, something that is important when you have projects and other work to get done.

Plan out meals

The time that you spend on meals can be enormous. If you are waiting until the last minute to figure out what is for supper, you are putting a lot of work on yourself. You might have to spend a lot of time trying to figure it out, going to the store to get the ingredients, and then still having to spend time getting it all done. Planning out the meals for a week can make things simpler. You can go out once and get all of the ingredients and then make it that night. It is even possible to make several meals at once to save even more time.

Learn personal time wasters

Everyone has something that they do that is going to waste time. This can include checking email, walking around the office, social media, or something else. Take a few minutes to determine what you do that waste time and then try as hard as possible to avoid doing it. Even avoiding it for an afternoon is going to save you a ton of time and you will be amazed at how much you can get done.

Travel Hacks

Travel can be a fun experience. However, if you do not prepare, it can be taxing and stressful. Exploring the unknown is more fun if you can just make the necessary preparations that will make your travel smoother and better. You will definitely benefit if you have prepared and ironed out everything, even before you board your plane.

There are a million things that could go wrong when you travel. Even seasoned travelers make mistakes too. Why endure making mistakes when you can prevent and avoid them in just a few easy steps?

Travel hackers are the people constantly chasing miles, rewards, points, and elite status. Do you think that you are a good travel hacker? Here are some tips that could help you.

Travel Hacks for Packing Your Things

Packing things can be such a chore. If you don't pack your things well, you might end up with excess baggage or you might forget something essential for your trip. Here are a few things that could make packing more convenient for you.

Make a checklist. Don't forget to pack everything that you need. If you are under any kind of medication, you must remember to pack enough medicines for your trip. You wouldn't want to go running around pharmacies, especially in a foreign country. It can be difficult to explain what you need, and dosages of their tablets might be different. Also, try to pack basic medicines for headaches, fever, and colds.

When you pack your clothes, you need to maximize space so that you won't have bulky luggage. Instead of folding your clothes, try rolling them, as this technique has proven to be very effective in saving space. Bring classic pieces and just mix and match when you are at your destination. Even if you are going to a tropical island for vacation, it is always a good idea to bring a nice dress or a smart casual outfit just in case something comes up.

A great tip is to take a photo of each suitcase while it's open so that you have an image of what's in each suitcase. That way, when you land you won't be searching for which suitcase has diapers—this is a great tip for traveling with kids!

If you are going for a short trip, you can use straws as containers for creams and liquids. Just make sure to seal them well and to put them in a zip lock to avoid making a mess in your luggage.

Travel Hacks before You Leave for a trip

Hotels are often pricey. If you are looking for something more affordable, try looking for a house for rent (if you are traveling with family) or a room for rent (if you are travelling alone).

Ever go on a long trip and come back and can't remember where the heck you parked your car? Take a quick photo with your smartphone BEFORE you leave the parking garage of which level and parking spot you used.

Make sure that you scan your passport, visa, and ticket, and e-mail them to yourself. You can also memorize your passport number and flight details if possible. This small step can save you from stress in case you lose these very important travel documents.

If you are going to a foreign-speaking country, search for apps that could help you to communicate with the locals. You don't need to learn the entire language. Choose apps wisely, and you will not have trouble conversing with locals about your basic needs.

When you plan to bring your camera, do not forget to take a picture of yourself first. It will prove that the camera is yours in case you lose it.

Travel Hacks during your trip

Train passes usually come cheaper if you book in advance. If you want, you can book everything in advance. Imagine the money you will save if you efficiently plan your itinerary ahead. All you have to do is to check the website of the train companies in the country you're visiting.

Take advantage of breakfast buffets. Fill up your tummy so that you won't spend much on food. Some food establishments even allow tourists to bring food when they leave. Take advantage of their generosity. More often than not, locals are more than happy to help tourists enjoy their trip.

Always remember the address of where you are staying. It is wise to bring a card of the hotel with you in case you get lost. You can always just show the card to someone, and it will be easier for you to find your way home.

While some countries often give tax rebates or discounts to tourists, there are vendors and sellers who will take advantage of tourists who are not informed of the proper pricing. Ask around and don't look like you will believe everything. As a traveler, you must always use caution to avoid scams and other sorts of trouble. Conversely, in Europe, be sure to look for a blue VAT FREE symbol in a shop—depending on the country and what you're buying, you could save 19% off the purchase price!

When you travel around tourist spots, one of the easiest ways to save money is to bring bottled water. You are bound to get thirsty often if you are always walking. Just refill your bottle whenever you get a chance.

It is a wise idea to use the internet for your own safety. Make sure that you search for any possible scams. Do your research. Blogs are very useful because they will tell you about the experiences. Read up before you leave. You never know when random information would come in handy. One great tip is to use the app City-Maps2Go—it's free and you can download a Google-based city map of most major cities. You don't need a data plan to run the app and it works as a GPS too! Plus, you'll have Wikipedia articles at your fingertips in the app so that you can do your own walking tour of the city.

Travelling can be very stressful if you are not prepared. However, if you efficiently plan out everything, you will likely minimize trouble.

Don't forget to have fun when you travel! Make friends and a lot of memories. As a frequent adventure seeker, I'm always looking for the best price, most memorable experiences and how to travel with the least amount of stress as possible. Over the years, I have uncovered tips and tricks the travel industry doesn't want you to know. I've condensed the best tips that will save you money and time, so you can focus on enjoying your adventure.

1. Get the Best Price on Airfare. The best time to purchase airline tickets is between six to eight weeks from your departure date. The only time you want to purchase tickets well in advance is if you will be traveling around or during major holidays.

Airfare rates can change up to three times a day. The best time to buy tickets is on Tuesday and Wednesday afternoons. If you have some flexibility when you can travel, that will help keep the costs down. Generally speaking, Sunday is the most expensive day to travel. The least expensive days to fly are Tuesdays, Wednesdays and Saturdays.

2. Find the Best Deal Possible by Becoming an Internet Ninja. Always enable private browsing when you are researching flights and hotels. Some websites will track your visit and raise the price slightly when they know you have visited before.

3. Roll Rather Than Fold. You can pack significantly more items in your suitcase by laying your clothes onto a flat surface and tightly rolling them up. This technique will also prevent wrinkling.

Stack as many as four of a like item (shirts, sweaters or pants, jeans) and roll them up. Stack heavier or harder items that have been rolled on the bottom part of your suitcase, towards the bottom part where the wheels are. Add the lighter items on top.

Shoes and wrinkle resistant items should go along the edges of the suitcase, creating a border of the rolled items. Cushion toiletries in a case or small bag on the top part of the suitcase with the softer rolls of clothes. Throw in a dryer sheet to keep your clothes smelling fresh while in transit.

4. Shoes Can Hold Items, Too. If you are pressed for space, pack your socks and undergarments into your shoes you will be carrying in your suitcase. I've also packed wine I've purchased at vineyards while on vacation into boots and slippers on my return flight home. They make for excellent cushioning!

5. Be Creative with Packing Small Items. Every time I am traveling and want to bring jewelry, I get pretty creative with how I pack them. Purchase a plastic weekly pill box and pack your earrings and rings in them for easy organization. For transporting necklaces hassle free, loop each chain on the necklace through a straw and make sure the clasp is closed. This will prevent tangling. Use disposable plastic contact lens holders to pack creams, liquid makeup and chapstick.

6. Create Instant Speakers in Your Hotel Room. You can easily turn up the volume of music, your alarm or a speaker phone by placing your phone into a ceramic mug (most hotel rooms have them available) in an upright position.

7. Know Your Options for Alternate Sources of Power. More than once I have forgotten my wall plug for my cell phone charger while traveling. And of course I didn't have my laptop with me, either. So I had to get clever. As long as you have the USB cable, you can charge it by plugging it into the USB slot of the television in your hotel room. This outlet will be located on the side of the screen or on the back.

8. Eat on the Cheap. If you are staying in a hotel that doesn't offer a free breakfast and you want to save on expenses, you can utilize some hotel room equipment to make food. Use the iron in your room to make paninis or grilled cheese. Build your sandwich of choice, wrap in foil and iron your sandwich on high for a couple minutes on each side or until your sandwich is golden brown and delicious.

You can also make instant oatmeal in your coffee pot. Simply add the instant oatmeal to the pot and allow the hot water to drip into the pot. Mix together well, add some nuts and berries and enjoy.

EVERYDAY HOUSEHOLD HACK HEROES

There are some items that have so many valuable benefits, that I wanted to create a special chapter just for these household heroes. These are seven items that are super cheap, have countless uses and should be the items you always have stocked in your pantry.

Let's take a look at these household heroes that will make your life incredibly easier and in some cases, will keep you healthier!

1. Lemons. Slice a lemon in half and squeeze the juice from one-half of the lemon into a cup. Add warm (or if you are like me, hot) water into the cup and drink it every morning. Not only does warm lemon water help you lose weight, it improves digestion, boosts your immune system, reduces inflammation, contains antibacterial and antiviral properties and boosts your brain power.

2. Epsom Salt. Epsom Salt is one of the most versatile items you can have in your home. While it is excellent for soaking in the bathtub to soothe sprains and strains, it can be used as a laxative and to cure pink eye. It's also useful for cleaning tile floors, bathtubs, removing burnt food from pots and pans, regenerating car batteries, and has multiple uses in gardening.

It can be used to draw out splinters, reduce inflammation, relieve gout pain, be used directly on bites and stings to relieve pain and can help eliminate blackheads. Epsom salt also has use in crafts, like creating snow and a frosted look on your windows in the winter. The uses of Epsom salt are endless, and it is super cheap. Keep a box or bag of it in your bathroom.

3. Coconut Oil. Coconut oil can be used in cooking, as beauty remedies, as toothpaste, lip balm and toothpaste. It can heal canker sores and season cast iron frying pans. This versatile oil can also be used as an insect repellant, can be used as a substitute for WD-40, as furniture polish, a leather shoe cleaner and to remove sticky residue from items. As an added bonus, substituting coconut oil for canola and vegetable oils can aid in weight loss.

4. White Vinegar. White vinegar offers some incredible cleaning properties. I always keep a large bottle of it in my home. To remove soap and scum build up from your shower head, simply add some vinegar to a bag and tie it around the shower head. Let it sit overnight and then run the shower in the morning. Your shower head will look brand new.

White vinegar can be used with baking soda to unclog and deodorize your drains. It can be used to disinfect cutting boards as well as steam clean your microwave when you combine it with water.

5. Toothpaste. Toothpaste is an excellent cleaning agent. You can use it to clean the leather part of your sneakers, clean fine jewelry and remove crayon marks from your walls. It can also be used to defog goggles and glasses, as well as to buff out small scratches on items. Toothpaste is also an amazing deodorizer for your hands when you can't get the smell of garlic off them, even after washing.

6. Coffee Filters. Even if you aren't a coffee drinker, coffee filters are cheap and have many issues. I use coffee filters as a mitt when cleaning windows, mirrors and wine glasses. They don't leave any streaks and are lint free. Using the filters in between expensive dinnerware when storing those helps prevent scratches and chips. They are also great to use at the bottom of flower pots because it prevents the soil from leaking out when watered.

7. Hydrogen Peroxide. Hydrogen peroxide has some great antibacterial properties that offer endless uses. I like using one part peroxide to one part water to use as a great disinfecting mouthwash. You can also combine it with baking soda to deep clean your teeth and whiten them.

Hydrogen peroxide can be used to disinfect cutting boards, dishwashers, sponges, toilets and bathtubs. You can also use a little in your sink with water to remove pesticides and dirt from fruits and veggies.

MEMORY HACKS

Have you ever been in an awkward situation wherein you do not know the name of the person you're talking to? Have you ever found yourself struggling to recall a phone number? Are you a student who is always struggling to recall the things that you studied? In this day and age, we are often offered too much information. Our constant struggle is in trying to remember everything.

When we were young, we had very sharp memories. However, as time goes by, most of us lose our ability to remember things efficiently. Memory is like a muscle, and it constantly needs to be exercised and used if you want it to be better and more efficient.

Ideally, writing down things and repeating them again and again is the easiest way to remember the details. However, we don't have this kind of luxury most of the time. There are times when you just have to think on your toes. You really don't need super powers if you want to remember passwords and client names. There are plenty of tools and techniques that can help you to remember things that you need.

Do not underestimate your brain! With the right amount of practice, you will be able to improve your memory habits in no time!

Here are some memory hacks, which you might find useful.

Rest and nap
How do you expect to recall things if your brain is never recharged? Getting sufficient rest and sleep ensures that your brain is able to process new material. Aside from getting your usual eight hours of sleep at night, you must also try to nap throughout the day. A simple fifteen minute nap can do wonders for your brain, and thus, for your memory as well.

While exercising your brain is important, you must give it time to rest too. Do not push your brain to the limits all the time. Working twenty hours a day will surely fry your brain cells. Just like any muscle, your brain needs regular rest and sleep too. Remembering things is rarely about being more intelligent. More often than not, it is about knowing how to use your brain properly in order to recall the information you need.

Here are some useful tips that could help you to have a sharper and better memory in general.

Learn how to focus

In this day and age, multi-tasking is a common buzzword. People often seem to find fulfillment in trying to achieve all things at once. However, this approach to things is very problematic. When you multitask, you make it difficult for yourself to understand. In addition to this, you don't fully absorb the information, which makes it difficult to recall and remember.

Remember keywords

Keywords can be very powerful in helping people to recall important information. When you encounter lengthy material like a history essay, take note of keywords to help you remember the things you want.

Choose powerful words that will enable you to remember a lot of information about the subject. Don't try to remember a lot of keywords, because it defeats the purpose of this technique. The key is to choose powerful ones that will unlock the core knowledge about the material that you are trying to remember.

Use repetition techniques

When you say something out loud, it will be easier for your brain to recall information. For example, when you are introduced to Gina, greet her with a phrase like, "Nice meeting you, Gina." Try to repeat the name multiple times in your conversation. Repeating the name again and again will embed it in your memory.

Use your own mnemonics

Mnemonics, or patterns of letters, words, or phrases, are a good way to remember things. If you use mnemonics, you are actually using your various senses to remember information. This makes it much easier for the brain to process and recall information. Use your own sense of humor to remember things well. Construct positive images that can help you to remember the important information that you need.

Train your brain

Train your brain to think more using exercises like puzzles and board games. Playing scrabble, crossword, and Sudoku could do wonders for your brain. You can also play memory games that will keep your brain working. The more you train your brain, the more efficient it will become. Simple games like these can even help prevent Alzheimer's and other brain diseases.

Engage your senses

The more senses you involve in learning something new, the easier it would be for you to remember important information later on. It would be best if you know what kind of learner you are. Some people learn faster through body movement. Some by imagining pictures. Some by singing songs. Figure out what your learning style is, and it will be significantly easier for you to recall information.

For visual learners, you can translate text into pictures. For auditory learners, you can assign a song or a tune, which can make learning faster and more efficient. Try to discover what kind of learner you are, so that you can maximize your own learning process.

Write it down

Whenever you have the luxury to write things down, go ahead and do so. This simple act embeds the important details into your memory. You don't actually have to read what you wrote down. The simple act of holding a pen and writing random notes engages brain cells, which make it easier for you to recall things that you might need later on.

Don't think that it is the same as typing away on a keyboard or touch screen. It is the act of writing, which makes things easier to remember because it engages your body. Sure, typing on a keyboard is faster and more convenient. Unfortunately, typing away does not engage the brain as much as writing does.

Exercise

By now, you should know that exercise has so many benefits. It is not just good for the body; it is good for the brain too. Your memory is sharper when you exercise, because exercise will allow you to free your mind from stress. With a clear mind, you will easily be able to retain important information.

TIPS FOR PLANNING

At some point in your life, you are going to have to plan. Whether this is for a party, an event, or for a trip you will need to make sure that everything is organized and that it can go off without any issues. Often events will fail because the proper planning did not go into them. Here are some of the things that you can do in order to use effective planning techniques.

Prioritize

Before you get started, you need to take the time to figure out what is the most important things that need to get done. Every morning, or before you go to bed for the night in order to clear your head, you should take the time to write out all of the things that you need to do the next day. You can then look at the list and determine what is the most important and needs to be taken care of as soon as possible. Mark those so that you know to do them first. Then look for the tasks that are still important but which can wait just a bit so that you can get the urgent ones done. And finally, have a category for the least important work that you will get to when you have the time later on. Keep in mind that not everything is urgent, no matter how you feel about the matter. Work through your list starting with urgent and ending with the lesser things if you have time. This will ensure that you get the work done that is needed on time instead of scrambling at the last minute because you worked on something else first.

Use the Tools You Have

Many people decide to use the tools they have online in order to be organized and to get things done. These tools are great because they provide you with easy access to all of the information that you need in order to get all of your work tasks done. For example, email is able to help you to send out the projects that you need and to keep in touch with those you are working with and you are probably already using it. Another feature that comes with a lot of email programs is the calendar feature. You should utilize this in order to keep track of projects, due dates, and appointments. The best part is that this calendar feature will send you email updates about what you have planned so you never forget anything.

Depending on the work that you are doing, there might be other tools that you can use to make work more efficient. For example, some comprehensive project management programs will allow you and others in your organization to work together on a project by sharing notes and other information.

Communication

You are never going to be able to get anything done if you do not have any open lines of communication available with those around you. Everyone will need to be informed on the project if you want it to get done the right way and on time. Communication will need to go both ways; if you have information on the project make sure to talk to others and share that information so that you are able to work together and get it done right. If you do not have information that is needed and feel like you are in the dark, make sure to talk to others on the team. They might have this information that can help you get going and contribute to the overall work. Communication can occur in several different ways. You can go to the other person's office to talk, call them, send an email, or even have meetings. The type of communication will vary depending on the scope of the project but the most important thing is to keep those lines open for everyone.

Make a Schedule

You are not going to be able to get anything done if you do not have any sort of schedule that is made up. A schedule is going to allow you to see what is going on each day, what tasks you will need to finish, and it allows you to plan out the day and the time that you have whether at home, the office, school, or somewhere else. If you do not create a schedule, things are going to get lost or you will jumble them up and soon too much will be on your plate or you will forget about things. In addition, if you are able to create a proper schedule, you will find that you can schedule your own down times. This time can be used to take a break, catch up on a project, or take on more work if you would like.

Make sure to that you take the time to work on a schedule, whether you plan out each hour of the day or just write it all down in a calendar. Having this schedule allows you to learn what to expect day to day and then you will be able to get it done, save time, and allocate tasks to certain times to get them done. For example, if you get to the office at 8 and have a meeting at 9, you might allocate your time to getting a few little important tasks done and can save the more in depth ones that need time for the afternoon when you have a few hours free.

WEIGHT LOSS AND EXERCISE HACK

1. Use Smaller Plate

Trick your mind into thinking that you've got a great big portion of food by using a smaller plate. This works because you'll be able to fit less on the plate while still having it look like a considerable amount.

Eating less is one of the hardest things to do, especially when you've been eating the same portion for a large number of years. You know what your plate looks like when it gets you full and thus, if you put less food on a bigger plate, you'll only crave more (because your mind already thinks it's not enough).

2. Walk more.

Those extra 2 minutes that it takes to get from the other end of the parking lot can make a huge difference. So, if you're the kind of person who tends to drive around until you find the closest spot in the parking lot, it's time to stop and drive to the farthest one. Additionally, you'll want to skip elevators and escalators and opt for the stairs.

3. Separate snacks into smaller portions.

If you're the type who pops a bag of chips open and finds it incredibly hard to put it down, it's time to start cutting down. It's hard to say kick the snacking all together, especially in the beginning stages and so, what you'll want to do instead is to put your treats in tiny Ziploc bags and toss away the big bag.

4. When at the park with your kids, get into play mode. Rather than only sitting around and watching to make sure that they're safe, engage them in a game of 'tag' and get your body up and moving.

5. When on vacation, don't leave your running shoes behind.

Sure you want to go sight-seeing and thus, you'll most likely be getting some walking in but the amount of walking you to will also be related to your comfort level when walking. Stress shoes and stilettos mean that you'll be taking the bus for what would only be a 10 minute walk.

6. Choose a day in the week to skip meat, soda or other edibles you'd like to cut down on.

7. Lose belly fat by drinking 5 cups of green tea daily.

8. Drink a cup of water before dinner to feel fuller faster.

9. Eating foods packed with Vitamin C reduces the production of Cortisol, which is a hormone responsible for the storage of body fat.

10. Pulling your tummy in while running or jogging will help you to tone it up a bit more and also burn more calories.

11. Burn more calories while you're asleep by enjoying a spoon of peanut butter before bedtime.

12. Invest in comfortable and attractive workout clothes. The better you look, the better you'll feel and the more you'll want to get suited up and out on the track.

13. Challenge yourself more with an activity monitor. Set realistic goals for yourself and push yourself to reach them.

14. Exercise while watching television. Choose your favorite television show and turn it into an exercising game. Whenever character X says a certain word, do 10 jumping jacks. Whenever another character laughs or cries, do 10 sit-ups.

15. Burn more calories by wearing a weight vest or backpack while walking or while running errands

Cut down the amount you eat by chewing more. This will allow you to truly enjoy your food and also prevent you from eating too much. Dinner isn't a race!

Google Tips and Tricks
If you are looking for tips on how to Google search, then you are on the right page

Here is the list of the tips you need to help you with Google searching.

1. Click on the "Advanced Search" for more specific searching.

a. Allows you to search exact phrases, "every word," or any of the keywords you specify. Just go to the appropriate box and enter the search terms.

b. Let you specify the number of results that you want to be shown on the current page, the language you prefer and the type of file you are looking for.

c. To limit the results, you can type in the box of the "Search within site of domain."

d. You can access more specific and advanced features when you click on the link of the "Date, Usage Rights, Numeric Range and More."

2. You can also find the advanced features on the front page of the Google search box.

3. Searching in google combines terms with the Boolean term "AND". So when you type water earth— it searches for water AND earth.

4. If you want to search for water or earth, just enter "water OR earth."

5. You can also use the symbol |, like this: "water | earth".

6. AND and OR are both case sensitive. They should be entered in upper case.

7. If you want to search for an exact term and then a keyword OR another term, you have to group them by using parenthesis, like this: earth (wind OR fire).

8. Quote the phrases that you are searching for, like this: " to be or not to be".

9. If you are looking for synonyms, use the symbol tilde before the keyword, like this, ":simple".

10. If you do not want to include exact keywords, use a minus operator, like this, "new laptops -eBay". This will not include eBay search results.

11. Google ignores "stop words," they are the common words such as I, like, if and then.

12. A plus operator assures that stop words be included in the search, for example "cookies +and chips"

13. A stop word will be included in your search if it is contained within a phrase between quotation marks.

14. Google can also fill in your search for example, "Thomas Alva Edison discovered*"

15. If you want to look for a numerical series use the operator for numrange. An example is searching for iPhone 6 prices between $1000 and $1200, enter, "iPhone 6 $1000..$1200"

16. Google recognizes many file types with the use of advanced search. Some of them are Lotus, Microsoft Office Document, Shockwave Flash, PostScript and ordinary text files.

17. You can search for a particular filetype using "filetype:[filetype extension]. For example, "basketball filetype:pdf".

18. You can omit the file types entirely by using the Boolean syntax that you used to omit key words, like "volleyball filetype:doc"

19. You can also combine any type of Boolean search options, just make sure that you have the correct syntax.

20. Google also has search parameters that are hidden like "intitle" which searches page titles only. For example, "intitle:vegetables".

21. The inurl modifier is used to search only the page's web address, try, "inurl:herbs".

22. To search for live webcams, use, "inurl:view/view.shtml".

23. If you only want to search for results in texts using page links, utilize the inanchor modifier.

24. To determine the number of links to a site, use, "link:sitename". An example is, "link:www.google.com".

25. To look for pages that Google thinks have related content, use, "related:modifier". An example is "related:www.yahoo.com".

26. To return information about a specific page, use the "info:site_name" modifier.

27. You can also use a typical search by clicking the "Similar Pages."

28. You can search for a specific site with the modifier "site:", an example is, "search pricelist site:www.amazon.com

29. You can access Google's database of rated and handpicked sites with the google directory using "directory.google.com".

30. The Boolean "intitle" and "inurl" and OR can also be used in the Google directory.

31. If you want to search for Google images go to "images.google.com"

32. Using the "source:" operator lets you choose specific archives.

33. The "location:" filter lets you get news which came from a particular country.

34. You can use "blogsearch.google.com" and also "inblogtitle:<keyword>"

35. To search for movie reviews, type in "movie:<name of film> or just use the "film:" modifier.

36. Type "showtimes" if you want to know the schedule and location where local films are shown.

37. You can also be specific with your search on a certain page, an example is, www.google.co.uk/movies

38. If you are searching for the director, enter "director:Big Hero 6"

39. If you are looking for the cast lists, enter "cast:name_of_film"

40. For music reviews, you can use, "music:name of band, song or the name of an album"

41. You can also get a 4-day forecast of the weather by using "weather <place/country/region>.

42. For the built-in dictionary, use, "define:<word>".

43. You can use "keyword cache:site_url" if you are searching for old sites contents. You can also use "cache:site_url".

44. For the built-in calculator, enter "12*15" and click on "Google Search."

45. You can also convert measurements and use natural language with the Google calculator, an example is, "140 stones in pounds."

46. Currency conversion is also supported, example is, "400 pounds in euro."

47. For more accurate results, you can enter the currency code, "500 GBP in EUR."

48. For temperature conversion, enter: "89 c to f" to convert Centigrade to Fahrenheit.

49. You can also search for the equivalent of Roman numerals, enter, "2468 in roman numerals."

50. You can create your own Google account by logging into www.google.com/account/ and then choose "Create Account.

a. You get a free email account on Google.
b. You can personalize your account's front page. You can add your blogs and feeds by clicking on the "iGoogle."

c. You can customize your tabs by clicking on "Add a Tab."

d. You can also have your own theme by clicking on the "Select Theme."

e. For you to gain access to all the Google sites and features, click on "Try something new." Then choose "More."

51. You can use "Custom Search" for an exclusive Google search.

52. You can do a personalized search by using "www.google.com/psearch."

a. It has a bookmark facility to let you save your bookmarks and access them anytime and anywhere that you like.
b. The iGoogle Bookmarks option can let you add and access your bookmarks.

53. You can look and search on your returned results by clicking on the link at the bottom of the page of your search results.

54. You can search for a map by adding "map" at the end of your search.

55. You can look for images by adding "image" at the end.

56. With the Google Image Search, you can look for recognized faces. Just type "&imgtype=face"

57. For information about stocks, type, "stocks:" and the market ticker of the company.

58. To search for the tracking information on a particular flight, just enter the flight number and carrier.

59. To determine the time at a particular place, enter "time" and then the name of the place.

60. There is a spell checker that is built-in which suggests alternative spellings for the term you use for searching.

61. You can use the "Translate Page" to see the results in English.

62. You can look for foreign sites by clicking on the "Language Tools" and then the country you prefer to translate your search.

63. There is also the translator on the language tools options.

64. You can also translate your text into your chosen language.

65. There is the "Search Preferences" option that you can use.

66. You can choose specific languages that you want your searches to have.

67. There is also your security from any explicit content; this is done by using the Google's Safe Search.

68. You can edit the number of items on your results page. You can use the default which is 10 and choose any number up to a hundred.

69. If you want to see what other people are looking for or if you want to improve your own page rank, go to www.google.com/zeitgeist.

70. For you to find the latest and most in-demand search terms, you can go to www.google.com/trends

71. You can compare two, three, or more terms by entering the terms in the trends' search box, separate them with commas.

72. Try typing "answer to life, the universe and everything" and wait for the result.

The next time you use Google, try to use and explore the tips and tricks stated above for you to experience them on your own.

HIDDEN HACKS OF VLC

VLC has heaps of features more than just a traffic cone icon that we are so accustomed. This segment unravels the versatility of this popular media player in simple step-by-step instructions.

Download YouTube Videos
VLC is your best friend when it comes to downloading videos from YouTube straight from its desktop interface. Here's how:

1. Search the video in YouTube and copy the path of that video from the address bar

2. Open VLC Media Player on your computer, open media, then paste the path then click play

3. Click "Tools" and choose "Codec Information"

4. Under "Location", you'll be able to see the download link, right-click this link and click "Select All" and copy the text to clipboard

5. Open a web browser and paste the link in the address bar. Press "Enter" key

6. Right-click anywhere on the browser window in which video is being played and select "Save As"

Recording clips from You Tube while it's streaming with VLC is also possible; just press the Red Record button in the player itself. This will allow you to have a snip out of a long video.

Record Your Desktop
VLC's flexibility extends to desktop recording as many of us find strange to know. VLC has the ability to record your desktop into a video file. It may not be as

power ful as to screen record an entire movie, but good enough to exhibit your desktop's activities into a video file. Here are the tips on how to do it:

1. Open VLC, Click Media

2. Choose Capture Device, select Desktop as the Capture Mode

3. Change the fps (frames per second). You may choose the 15 fps for desktop recording but for a fast-paced movement, 30 fps will be required. Make sure the source is your screen.

4. Click Next to "Play" and select "Convert"

5. From "Profile" dropdown, choose MP4 (You can use the tool icon to modify the settings of this profile)

6. In the destination box, choose a location to place the finished file

7. Stream by clicking "start"
VLC will now start to capture your desktop's feed in which anytime you want to stop recording, just click the stop button on your VLC. The desktop recording can be played as common media files.

Convert Video Files
One of the many facets of VLC is converting videos to certain formats, no need to download another application just to convert the file. This saves you the hassle of having different applications for certain file format. Learn how:

1. Click on 'Media" then click Convert/Save

2. From the "Settings" section, Choose the type of file you want to convert the file into

3. Choose a name for the file and location under Destination

4. Click on the "Start" button

Record Your Webcam

VLC gives you the luxury of taking pictures and recording them even if your webcam does not have the software to do so. VLC presents you a wide array of formats and settings to choose from, which makes it a vital tool in recording You Tube videos. Let me tell you how.

1. In VLC, open Media then Click Open Capture Device

2. In the" Capture mode" dropdown, choose Direct Show

3. Under "Video Device Name" choose your webcam

4. Under "Audio Device Name" choose your microphone

5. Click 'Advance Options"

a. If your webcam has a software that you opt to use, choose "Device Properties"

b. Or, you may enter a value for "Video input frame rate". 30 is best for crisp video quality

c. Click "Okay"

After the steps above, you now have two choices: You can press "Play" to watch live video through VLC and record segments by pressing "Record" button. Another is to select "Convert/Save" and select the location where you would like to save the recorded file. Both options have features that are suitable to your needs. If you want to preview your video and take short clips, use the first option. One tip to get rid of feedback problem is to use a headphone. Please take note though that this method will not give pitch perfect recording on slower computers.

 "Convert/Save" method is one way of avoiding any feedback problem; furthermore, it doesn't show visibility of the video being recorded or any of the recording status. You can stop the recording by pressing "Stop" but there's no indication status shown after doing so.

Subscribe to Podcasts

Podcast is an awesome way of listening to music or radio over the internet and VLC lets you subscribe to your favorite podcast online. Let's learn how:

1. Search for podcasts available, pick one and copy the website address

2. Click the plus sign beside the podcast label, then enter the URL that you copied.

3. Click on the podcast subscription you added, select and play a podcast episode.

VLC is more than just a media player. It encompasses a comprehensive range of technological advancements all rolled into one. It is indeed an absolute advantage for someone to know the best hidden features of VLC and have cutting-edge skill that's a cut above the rest.

Clever Gadget Hacks

I. Out of the box Desk Organizer

Who could ever imagine that a broom head can be used as an organizer? If you are a shrewd stylist who can come up with just about anything and everything under the sun, you will be able to think of the idea. For other people, it would be really hard.

Are you thinking of a unique, hand crafted and inventive gift to family and friends? Here is an awesome gift suggestion to consider before you head to your favorite department store.

1. You will just need these practical and affordable items available at the nearest hardware or janitorial stores:

- 2 Broom heads sizes 10" x 2.75"
- Your phone's charging cable
- 8 Stick-on Rubber feet
- Scissors

2. Placing the rubber feet

- On the wooden handle, bottom part of the broom heads, stick rubber feet on all corners with at least ¼" from the edges.

3. Creating your mobile phone's charging slot

- Find the built-in spaces amongst the broom's bristles, this will house your phone while charging, do this in just one of the broom head. Trim the bristles in a manner that will allow your phone to be settled evenly in that space.   Do this by ensuring that bristles will be cut fittingly.

4. Wire Connections

- Insert the other end of your phone's charger into the hole that has the thread. Just leave the charging port that connects to your phone at the bristle tops.

5. Put them all together

- Voila! You now have a distinctive desk organizer that you can place beside your desktop or workstation. Just make sure that it is close to a power source for your mobile phone charging needs.

II. RC Power Wheels

In today's advancing technology, reinventing a remote control power wheel may just be a little tougher than what it is like in the past. It requires basic mechanical knowledge to allow you to tweak the electrical wiring connections correctly and adjust it to your needs.

One good example of RC power wheel realignment is the one designed for a child with cerebral palsy. The RC power vehicle is altered and enhanced to match the limited movements of the child. The companion controls the RC system while the child rides his jeep by himself. The system set up costs roughly $1,000. A measly amount compared to the happiness it gives to the child.

III. Easy to Do Robot Gripper

Soon – gone are the days of manual human labor as the time of mechanically engineered agents or robots are proliferating in this time and age. These robots may come with a highly complex mechanism or may just be composed of plain and simple mechanical components. Scientists and researchers have come up with different kinds of robot grippers or end effectors, all of which have different functions.

These end effectors have varying mechanisms to mimic the hand movements of humans. All of the end effectors have a common mechanism as follows: Gripper approaches an object in a soft state. Gripper takes the shape of the object being picked up, and air is pressurized so objects can be manipulated. Let's take a look at an example of an amorphous robot gripper where we are going to use the jamming process.

We will need these materials to do our amorphous gripper:

Balloons, coffee grounds, plastic funnel, air hose/tubing, duct tape, small plastic tube, air pump and thin cloth.

The Jamming Process:
The coffee grounds are placed inside the balloon; there is an air hose that serves as the passage of air from the air pump. When you start to release air from the balloon, the coffee grounds will loosen up. Now when you press it against any object, the coffee grounds will circulate inside the balloon, allowing them to take the form of the object. This movement will let you hold an object by pressing hard against it and then extracting air from the balloon. The balloon's rubberized surface aids in gripping the object for it not to slip.

IV. iTorch Raspberry Pi Flashlight Projector
Expand your viewing pleasure with a portable and wireless projection system that will allow you to project your media wherever you may be. It combines the capabilities of a viewing device and a controller with the use of a battery powered projector. It is illuminated by a flashlight which can be a costly project but this innovation will allow you to project holograms anywhere you like.

V. Cheap Lithium Battery Pack
Converting your old mobile phone battery into a lithium battery is one of the highly clever hacks nowadays. For one, lithium-polymer battery packs are expensive since these are one of the advanced and powerful batteries today.
It takes a skillful mind to do this project because this is highly sensitive and risky procedures are involved. Make sure you equip yourself with the right steps and precautionary measures before embarking on this plan.

VI. Arduino Thermostat

Living in the small confinements of an apartment or dorm can be painstaking, especially to those who are living in cold places. Using an Arduino thermostat, temperature sensor and a motor will help ease the burden of manually switching your heater on/off to your desired temperature.

VII. 3D Scanning with Skanect

Would you like to see a mini me of yourself? Here comes 3D Scanning using the Microsoft Kinect and Skanect software.

1. To do this, you will need the following: desktop since the files are large, Skanect software (http://skanect.manctl.com/). Microsoft Kinect, lights and spinning platform

2. For the software settings: inside Skanect, click New, make sure that your settings match those in the picture. Press start – for small figure. You will need to adjust the bounding box a bit smaller.

3. For Workspace: Screen will show the bounding box in the middle. The infrared light and the video images are on the right side.

4. For Image: Have your subject step on the platform; make sure that the lighting is just right and consistently focused on your subject.

5. Kinect : One needs to hold the Kinect up as the level of the subject's waist, press record. The Kinect will record the depth and the color.

6. Movement: Spin Around – As soon as you have a full sweep of your subject, press the pedal to make the platform spin. As your subject is spinning, scan his entirety to capture the figure from head to toe.

VIII. Controllable Coffee Roaster From an Air Popcorn Popper

Coffee lovers will appreciate DIY Coffee Roaster. It needs basic engineering and craftsmanship to transform a hot air popcorn popper into a functional coffee roaster.

All you need is a proper adaptation of internal temperature sensors along with the reactive control system and the software's ability to save the roasting profile. This DIY will definitely match the expensive programmable roaster.

These clever gadget hacks will greatly help you survive in this modern age. These are inventive techniques that can help alleviate the conundrum of our daily living. If you just have the time, equipment, software and a little bit of craftsmanship then you can absolutely experiment on doing these suggestions and see how it is to live life in innovation.

MACBOOK HACKS

The following is applicable to all the users of the latest OS X version which you may download free from the App store.

Moving on. Here is the list of 35 MacBook hacks you need to know.

1. Copying & Pasting. Highlight the text, then hit Command + Shift + C to copy and Command + Shift + V to paste.

2. Special Character Use. Holding down the key for a few seconds after typing "e" or "i " will get you a list of special characters.

3. Finding Definitions. Navigate your cursor over any word then hit Command + Control + D and a definition will pop out.

4. Inverting Colors. Hit Command + Option + Control + 8 and you automatically invert the color on your screen. On Mountain Lion, this was formerly disabled. To turn this on, go to System Preferences > Keyboard > Shortcuts > Accessibility then click the "Invert Colors" box.

5. Zooming. Pressing Command + Option + 8 allows you to zoom through a page to the max. For finer zooming, press Command + Option + (=). Pressing Command + Option + (-) zooms you out of the page.

6. Purging. Do you notice that your computer is starting to respond slowly? Maybe it's time to clean it up to free some space. Take note that this works only with OS 10.7 or higher. In the Terminal app command line, type "Purge" and at least 500MB of space will be available for you.

7. Menu Bar Date and Time Icons. Go to System Preferences > Date and Time > Clock then check "Show Date" option under "Date Options." This will add to the menu bar the time, date, and battery percentage. If you wish, you may also add the day of the week, a clock icon, and so on.

8. Menu Bar Battery Life Icon. If you want your battery life status to be shown, just tick the battery icon then the "Show Percentage" option.

9. Adjusting Brightness & Volume. Press Shift + Option then press the volume and brightness buttons to your desired adjustment.

10. Choosing a Quiet Startup. If you don't want the sound that your computer makes when starting up, just hit F10 or the mute button.

11. Controlling Volume Sound. To turn the sound up or down, just click and hold Shift + the volume key.

12. Tweeting. While logged in your Twitter account using your Mac, send tweets simply by selecting any text, right click, and then click "Tweet."

13. Deleting. To delete letters in front, hit the fn key + delete. To delete the last typed word, press option + delete.

14. Mouse Trackpad Use. There's a lot you can do with this trackpad of your Mac computer which will make life so much easier for you. These includes smart zoom, zooming, and rotating among others. To figure them out, click System Preferences > Trackpad then navigate those tabs. Changing your trackpad's speed is an option for you also.

15. Saving Energy. Save your computer's battery life with this feature. You may choose to put your hard disk to sleep or set up a sleep time schedule by going to System Preferences > Energy Saver.

16. Use of Hot Corners. This is one cool trick your Mac can do. It lets you do a task by simply navigating through each of the four corners of your screen. To illustrate, scrolling to the bottom left of your computer screen may make your display go to sleep, launch Dashboard, etc. To activate this, you have two options. One is to go to System Preferences > Mission Control > Hot Corners. The other option is to type "Hot Corners" into spotlight search.

17. View Change. Press the Command key + 1-4 to modify view options when doing a finder window search.

18. Using Spotlight Math. Your Mac can help you solve your Math problems by using the calculator app without having to open it. Just input your Math problem into your spotlight search and it will give you the solution.

19. Changing Icon Size. To manually adjust app icon size, hit Command + J after selecting an app in the finder window.

20. Hiding Your Dock. If you want to get rid of the dock, click Command + Option + D. To bring it back, just press those keys again.

21. Hiding Your Apps. To instantly hide the apps you are currently using, click Command + H. To hide all the apps that are open, click Command + Option + H. To minimize the app you're in, click Command + Option + M. These commands won't get rid of the app's sound, though, so if you want to log out of them, just click Command + Option + Q.

22. Saved Document Search. Forgot where you saved a document you worked on? Clicking the icon on top of an open app will help you find it.

23. Using Finder Window. If your finder window is too crowded, you may press Command + Option + S. Doing this will make the finder sidebar collapse and let you concentrate on what you want to search for.

24. Path Bar Use. When you want to know where exactly a file you are looking for is use the finder window. Hit View and "Show Path Bar" to display in the windows a list of your path.

25. Navigating Between App Windows. If you have several windows open in an app, type Command + ~ to navigate between those.

26. Set Sound. On your computer screen's top right you can find the sound icon.

Click the Option key then the sound icon if you want your sound settings change.

27. Menu Bar Cleanup. Pressing the Command key and the app icon then dragging it away from the menu bar will get rid of litter you no longer use. This is not applicable to third party applications though.

28. Using Force Quit. Right click on the app icon then press "Force Quit" if it suddenly stops responding. Hitting Command + Option + Escape opens up the Force Quit menu, wherein you may choose to force stop any or all of your apps that are currently running.

29. Killing Widgets. You may have lots of widgets all running at the same time. You can find them in the Apple's OS widgets page. These can suck up a lot of your battery life, which you most likely want to save. To do this, go to the widgets page and hit the x in each running widget's corner.

30. Creating Text Shortcuts. This is like a word expander feature which is very helpful if you type a lot. To add text shortcuts, go to System Preferences > Keyboard > Text.

31. Screencast Recording. Want to record your screen's activity? You can do so by opening QuickTime Player and choosing New Screening Recording from the menu. To pick the audio source, click the drop-down arrow. You may also opt to show the mouse clicks and choose recording in either full screen or not.

32. Document Signing. You may now add your signature to any document. This is especially true in OS X 10.7 using Preview. In Preview's preferences, click Signatures then the + sign. Check the "Save this signature option". Get a piece of paper, put your signature, and hold it facing the webcam. Line it up then click Accept.

33. Speeding up Bookmarks Bar. Each bookmarked website placed in the bookmarks bar using safari creates a keyboard shortcut. To open the first site in the bar, press Command + 1, Command + 2 for the second, and so on.

34. iTunes Library Music. Sharing your music on your Mac is very easy. You may choose to share it with everyone by going to iTunes > Preferences > Sharing then check the "Share my library on my local network" option. At the bottom, there is a box wherein you can set a password if you want to limit it to certain users.

35. Password Retrieval. Forgot your password? Relax. Your Mac may just have saved it. If you want to look for a certain website, go to Utilities then run Keychain Access. Right click on that website then choose "Copy Password to Clipboard." To verify your identity, you may need to input your user login password. The forgotten password will then be duplicated, which you can now use to log in.

ANDROID HACKS

One of the marvels of today's technology is the advent of smart phones. They made our lives convenient, inventive and progressive. This article will guide you on the benefits of your smart phones as well as unravel its unknown features. Functionalities reserved for your smart phones that are capable of handling social networking, music and security will be presented to you. Also included are the hacks for smart phone users' wide array of features for phone, camera, spreadsheets, maps, music and almost everything under the sun.

To sum it all off, you will be guided on how to get the most of owning a smart phone device and walk you through the Android Market where you can choose from a vast array of free games and applications.

Below are the tips and tricks on how you can have the best features of your smart phones:

1. Check the permissions. Make it a habit to read through the apps permission before you even click the accept button as most of them requires access to your contacts.

2. Protect Battery Life. Be wary of your battery usage as it is easily drained every time you use an app or a game. For tips about battery performance enhancement, you may check out the app JuiceDefender. It will show you the tasks and make the most out of your battery charging.

3. A Smarter Keyboard. This may be unheard of for most of the android user but you can enhance the keyboard experience of your smart phone thru an app available for free in the app store. This is called Smart Key board Pro. This will give you the same performance with that of iPhone's keyboard.

4. Check the Speed. To test your smart phone's data speed, you can always rely on the app called Speedtest.net. This will provide you an accurate data of your phone's internet connection speed.

5. Batteries and Wi-Fi. Contrary to the popular notion that your Wi-Fi connectivity will drain your battery, the truth is it will actually lengthen its usage. Try to set your Wi-Fi router to on or enabled and see it for yourself.

Tips for travelers

1. Power. One of the travelers' outmost concerns is the power and where they will get it in case they run out of it. Some of the options are just at the tip of your nose like the car charger, solar power, emergency battery and power banks.

2. Mobile costs. It is always advisable to check out the best SIM promo if you will go out of the country. Always check data charges before going on a trip.

3. Protection. One of the first things that you should consider upon acquiring your phone is how to protect it physically. Encasing it is one; choose a phone case that is shock-proof as well as water-proof. So that in case something happens to your phone, you don't have to worry about the physical and internal damage.

4. Plan Ahead. For people who are always on the go, a very helpful app to help you through is TripAdvisor. This app is your friend when it comes to planning a trip, booking a hotel, setting time zones, as well as giving you a heads up of the places that you plan to visit by showing you photos and maps of that place.

FACEBOOK HACKS

Facebook can be considered as one of the most famous websites in the internet today. Most people visit the site every day. Some of them visit the site, a couple of times a day and there are those who are most of the time online on Facebook. Navigating through Facebook is a little complicated to some people because the simplest activities seem to be difficult to operate. To help you with your Facebook concerns such as editing and setting up its different parts, follow the list below. Most people are unaware of the following strategies. If you continue reading, you would be lucky enough to learn these simple techniques on how to manipulate your Facebook account.

1. Embed post
You will see an arrow pointing downwards on the top-right corner of the post. The drop-down menu will show you a list and at the bottom you will find the "Embed Post." Click it for you to get the embed code. Visitors of your page can also like your page by clicking on the embedded post.

2. Schedule your post
While composing your post, you can schedule the exact time and date you want your post to be published. On the lower left corner of your post, you will find the clock button, just click it and the option to schedule the time and date will appear.

You can also try this application. If you are a working or a busy person but you still want to appear active with your posts, the app Buffer is applicable to you. You can now schedule your posts at different times of the day. By using this app, you will never fail to be present, especially when your posts are important.

3. The best time to post
Do you want to know the best time to post on your page? Worry no more, because Facebook can track the time your fans are online. Go to the "Page Insights", part of your page. You will see the "Posts" tab, click it and then select the tab "When your

fans are online." You will find a graph showing the information regarding the days and times most of your fans are online. To easily get their attention with your post and to make sure that they don't miss reading your post, pick those times wherein most of your fans are online.

4. Posting to Specific Fans

If you want to let a specific audience see your post, click on the target button and you will see a drop-down menu of the specific audience you might want to choose. There are many options that will appear, just choose what you like while you are composing your post.

5. Editing Posts

To easily edit your post, just click on the downward arrow on the top-right corner of your post and click on "edit". This will help you edit your post, no need to delete or repost.

6. Facebook pages Manager App

The Facebook Pages Manager App is now available at the App Store. With this app, you can easily manage your page using your smartphone. You don't have to be sitting all day using your desktop or laptop while managing your pages.

7. Posting to Specific Languages

To make your post visible to your international viewers, just click on the "Target" button while you are in the process of composing your post. A dropdown menu will show you a list. Scroll down to the "Language" button, and then choose "All languages." There will be a popup menu wherein you can enter the specific language that you like. Your international customers will easily understand your post. There is no need to use "translation". This way, you can easily market your product or anything about your page. Communication is the key and language is the tool for it.

8. New pages to watch

To easily track your friends or competitors, you can go to the "Add pages" located in the "pages to watch" section of your Admin panel. This will allow you to track up to five (5) pages. It also allows you to keep track of the "likes" on your page.

9. Highlight important posts

To highlight your post, click on the down arrow that you will find on the top-right corner of your post, scroll down to the "Highlight" button. This will enable people to always see your post.

10. Editing your relationship status

There are times when you want the change of your relationship be a secret to your friends. This is because it is awkward to share with your friends that you are now single. To avoid this, you can go to the "About" section on your own timeline. A dropdown will appear, choose the "Relationship" section. Click on the "Edit" button located on the top-right corner and change your privacy settings to "Only Me." Continue to edit your new status and then save your work.

Another case is when you don't want a relationship status to be seen on your timeline. Go to the post about your relationship status and then choose "Edit" or "Remove" and then click on the "Hide from Timeline" option. The post will not be seen both on your own timeline and your friends' newsfeeds.

11. Sending Facebook Messages without downloading the Messenger App

You can easily chat and send messages to your friends in your Facebook browser alone. There is no need for you to download the Messenger App, saving you from using up space on your storage.

12. Post to Facebook even if you are not online

A "post-by-email" address will let you post on Facebook without actually being online. This will help you update your friends with your activities when you have a poor internet connection or while you're travelling. To find this address, go to any Facebook page. Click on the down arrow and a dropdown menu will appear, click on "Settings." Choose the "Mobile" option. There you will see your very own "post-by-email address." Before using the address, make sure that you have already added your phone number to receive Facebook texts.

Once you use the address and you do not have any photos or videos, the email subject that you input will be the status posted on your timeline. You can also add a caption to the photo or video you uploaded by using the subject in your email. You can easily change the privacy setting of your uploaded photos or video.

13. Disabling the "Seen" on your messages

If you are not yet ready to reply to messages and you don't want your friends to see that you have already read their messages, you can opt to turn the "seen by" or "seen on". For Google Chrome users, you can try the "Facebook Unseen" extension. For non-Chrome users, you can try installing a browser extension for AdBlock Plus. After installation, include this URL to the extension's custom filters- "facebook.com/ajax/mercury/change_read_status.php$xmlhttprequest." There are still other options that you can find in the "StackExchange thread."

14. Using Emojis

Emojis are those smileys or emoticons that are used in Japanese electronic messages. You can always add emojis in your status posts and comments. This can be used with both desktop and smartphones. For desktop users, you can download a browser extension for emojis like "ShowMeEmoji Chrome extension". For mobile users, you can use the emoji keyboard. You can also copy paste the emojis.

One way for your comments to be noticed is by using smileys that are relevant to your posts. This can be done easily with the use of Alt codes. Just press the "Alt" key followed by any number. This will create different symbols that you can use.

15. Using the Friend Tracker

Using the friend tracker "Nearby Friends" is a Facebook feature that lets you know your friends in the same area as yours. If you use this your friends who are in the same area will get notified and the other way around. It uses the GPS location to track your friends. Be aware, that this feature is optional. You and your friends must have this feature in order for you to keep track of your locations.

The location can also be available for your specific group like family, friends or colleagues. It can also let you know the nearness of your friends in miles (one mile or ½ mile, and so on). You can also choose to share your exact location. Clicking on the arrow button beside your friends' name can let you choose how long they can see your location and also add a note.

16.Stopping Facebook Ads
Facebook ads can sometimes be annoying so you can choose to stop them from appearing on your newsfeed. You can choose to turn off tracking through the app itself or you can adjust preferences.

17. Using Facebook Graph Search
If you like to search for specific photos or things about your friends, you can choose to use the Facebook Graph Search. Just type in specific things or persons you are looking for and you will be glad to see the results.

18. Posting GIF
Giphy search engine for GIF can be used to post GIF images to Facebook. You go to the site of Giphy, choose a GIF that you like to post, copy and paste the URL into your status. An auto-generated link with a play button will appear on the image preview just like a video.

19. Doing a Privacy Checkup
To help you with editing your settings you can use the Privacy Checkup Option on your page. This is a new feature that will help you review and edit your settings. Even if you have been using Facebook for a long time, there are still times when you get confused with the options or steps in editing certain parts of it.

20. Receiving an SMS login notification
For security purposes, you can choose to activate the login notification of SMS of your account. You can receive a notification of the device details, together with the exact time and date every time you log in to Facebook. To do this, go the "Account Settings" section, choose "Security Settings." When you see the "Login

Notifications," click it. Tick on the check box for "Text Message." The "Mobile Settings" section is where you register your cellphone number. Don't forget to register your mobile number on the "Mobile Settings" section before enabling the Text Message Notification.

21. Including profile pictures on chat

Aside from smileys, emojis and symbols, you can as well include profile pictures on your chat messages. You can use your own profile picture or anyone else's or even any Facebook Page's username. The URL which is located in the address bar contains the username, you simply have to copy and then paste the username in the chatbox. After identifying the username, you have to enclose the name in double pairs of braces. For example, [[name]] or [[yourname]] or [[facebookpage]].

22. Downloading a friend's photo album together with the comments

An application that you can use to download an entire photo album together with the comments is the Photo Grabber. If you would like to view a certain photo album offline, you can always use this app. However, if you just want the images to be downloaded, the Pic&Zip application will work right for you. Facebook videos can also be downloaded with this app.

23. Auto-zooming images

You can enjoy and appreciate looking at images/photos in full size by just hovering your mouse on the image that you like. For Chrome users, install the "Hover Zoom" extension on your browser. Firefox users can use Thumbnail Zoom.

24. Playing a prank

You can now pretend to be using a Blackberry or any iPhone model. You go to the link http://apps.facebook.com/viabberry/ and pick which device you want. Even if you are using a different device, your friends can see "Posted via Blackberry" or "Posted via iPhone."

25. Starting Group Chat

For you to start a group chat, you just need to open a chat box of any online friend, choose "Gears" and then "Add Friends." Just enter the names of your friends that you wish to include in the chat. After adding your friends' names just click "Done."

26. Making money while sharing

If you want to earn money while online, you can join several websites. One site that you can sign up is Wingsplay. On this site, you will be sharing videos. Be sure to ask your friends to watch the videos you post because your earnings depend on the hits. You can also share those videos to other social media sites like Twitter and your Blog Page, if you have any. You will not only be only entertained but you also earn as well.

27. Logging-out automatically

You might be always forgetting to sign out of your Facebook account. This can lead to some problems, especially when somebody tries to use your account and pretends to be you. For Chrome users, you can simply choose to use the Facebook Auto-Logout extension. This will enable you to log out your Facebook on the specific time that you schedule it. Another option to secure your privacy for Chrome users is by creating multiple accounts. This way, your important data, passwords and browsing history is safe.

28. Taking part in a movie

Lollipop is now the world's fastest growing interactive short film app that is available on Facebook. Here, you will take the role as a "Wanted." A skinny frightening character will search for your location.

29. Appearing Offline to some friends

If you want to appear offline to some friends who keeps on bugging you through chat, it is now possible to block them. From your chat bar, choose the "Settings Gear Icon" and then choose "Advanced Settings." You can now type the names of your friends with whom you want to be offline. Now, you can be free from disturbances.

How to Make Your Post Appear on Top of the Newsfeed

Are you wondering why there are posts that are always on top of your newsfeed? No matter how many new statuses your friends post, there are some which remains on the top spot of your newsfeed. Time and time again, Facebook tries to come up with new ways to make some posts become more visible. With the aid of today's modern technology, Facebook has developed a way in which it is able to identify the posts that it thinks is important. If you want yours to always stay on top, there are ways to achieve that.

1. Congratulating someone

If you want your post to be seen by all, try posting a message congratulating someone. Positive vibes is very obvious when it comes to greeting someone or congratulating those who celebrated memorable events in their lives like birthdays, anniversaries, wedding, graduation, and so on and so forth. This is the reason why Facebook feels and thinks that people would love to view such posts, so, Facebook made it possible to make those posts more visible to the subscribers.

2. Refrain from asking for Likes and/or Shares

It is not really that entertaining to see posts begging for likes, shares or comments, so Facebook came up with the method wherein posts as such be eliminated from newsfeeds.

3. Make your posts interesting

Your posts will gain more views, likes and shares if you post something interesting that will catch your friends' attention. If you do this, your post will most likely stay on top. You don't have to beg for likes if you do this.

4. Sharing information about trending topics

You can increase the chance of seeing your post that shares some information about a trending topic. Viewers will be interested in topics that are viral because it easily get their attention. To put your post on top of the news feed, try to posts trending topics which will the interest of a wide range of people.

5. Including links

The developed method of Facebook works in a way that it acknowledges posts which includes links to several web pages. For Facebook, this is a sign that you have done some research on the topic, making it more important than other posts. Copy and paste works wonders.

6. Don't using negative language.

You should avoid using words that show or express negative feelings such as anger, stress, disappointment and the likes. Facebook prefers positive feeling over negative ones. Posts which use angry words are less likely to appear on newsfeeds.

7. Upload a number of pictures in your post

With Facebook's method, uploading multiple pictures in one post mean that the event is important. Friends and viewers will see those types of posts in their walls.

8. Schedule your post during regular hours

During weekdays, most people are online during regular hours so this is the best time to post. Weekends especially during Saturdays are also a good time to post and be seen.

9. Log in regularly

Frequent users are given more priority to be seen than those who goes online occasionally. It will do you good if you log in and post constantly.

Upon discussing all the tips you can now analyze that Facebook recognizes and gives more value to posts that it thinks are appealing to the viewers.

EVERNOTE HACKS

Evernote is a very useful tool. Often times it is defined as a tool for note-taking but there is more to it than that. It has a lot of functions to help you. People from all walks of life can benefit from it especially those business executives and content marketers who deal with great quantities of information. It helps you create and access your notes in plain text form, audio, video and Web clippings. You can also access those anywhere with the use of the Web or different mobile and desktop applications.

Here, you will find the best features of Evernote. Some tips and tricks are also included. You will learn a lot and you will be able to maximize your Evernote experience with all this information.

Best Features

1. Transcribing your voice with the Voice2Note by Dial2Do application

You can record your voice notes with EverNote. With Voice2Note by Dial2Do, audio notes can be converted into text, this way it becomes more searchable. Just connect your account; the first thirty seconds of your audio note will be recorded. You can also tag someone by saying "tag with:" and then the name of the people that you will tag. You can try the free version or choose to have the upgraded and advanced versions with the annual or monthly fee.

2. Sending photos right from the camera with the Eye-fi

Eye-fi is a gadget that can make your device be Wi-Fi enabled, you can insert into the slot of your camera or Digital SLR's SD card. With Eye-fi, images can be directly sent as picture notes. You can capture text from menus, signs, and other sites and then send them to Evernote in an editable and searchable form.

3. Saving other people's tweets with the Twipple

If you don't have time to respond to tweets, you can save those tweets to your notebooks and tag them. This allows you to go back to them.

4. Scanning documents

There are several manufacturers offering the integration of Evernote to their scanners. With Ricoh, Doxie, Fujitsu, Lexmark and Canon, you can send scanned documents directly to your account.

5. Tweeting directly to Evernote

You can tweet short notes directly to Evernote. You just have to Follow @myEN. It will then follow you and will allow you to get to your Twitter then to EverNote. Just include "@myEN" to your tweet and send a DM to the account. It can also be used to remember the tweet of others by retweeting them and adding @my EN at the end of your tweet.

6.Saving audio, drawings and handwritten notes with the Livescribe smartpens

The Livescribe smartpens are gadgets that keep digital records of the items that you draw and write with. They can also save audios. With these, everything that you've heard and written can be archived and sent to your account.

7. Taking notes with the FastFinga app

FastFinga is an iOs app that lets you write by using your fingers on your gadgets screen. If you have connected your account, you can easily send notes directly to your Evernote.

8. Adding city guides, puzzles, and other things to your EverNote account

EverNote has a wide selection of free notebooks that offer free reading materials such as short city guides, recipes, puzzles and a whole lot more.

9. Saving articles with ReadItLater

ReadItLater is an iOs application that lets you copy a version of a particular webpage with just a click. It also has an option that lets you share pages to EverNote. It is useful especially if you want to have an archive of the most popular pages in your filing system.

10. Emailing notes directly to your account

Emailing is the easiest way to send any content to your account. The Account

Settings contain the email address. By simply typing @notebook in your subject, you can also add notes to a particular notebook. You can also tag notes by entering #tag in the subject.

You can maximize the functions of EverNote by having more notes. It becomes more useful if you have a lot of information.

Useful Tips to Maximize EverNote Functions

1. Creating synchronized notebooks

If you have a coordinated notebook, you will be able to jot down notes and continue what you are doing on whatever device you prefer.

2. Using the Web Clipper

You can clip the contents of a webpage together with their links and images and add some notes to be used later. This feature can also work with Google especially when you are researching.

3. Using note links to work on related articles

If you are working on a project and you have different articles related to your topic, you can create the outline of your topic. You just copy the link of your note and then paste it to a different note to enable you to connect it to the first article you have.

4. You can put important notes in your EverNote toolbar.

You don't have to check and shift through all your notes because it is already available in your toolbar.

5. Saving handwritten notes into ink notes

Open Ink Note. You can use a pencil or a pen to start drawing or writing. You can also include your signature.

6. Mailing your note to your account

You can send a note to yourself with the use of any email. Upon signing up to EverNote, you will be given your own EverNote account.

7. Using "EverNote Clearly"

This is considered to be one of Accessibility's best tool. It allows you to highlight any text on webpages; clip parts of the page's content and also save them; edit the font size and theme of a particular page; print according to your preferred font and theme; and be able to convert the texts into speech in different languages (this particular function is not free).

"EverNote Essentials" Tricks to Improve Productivity
1. Naming your default notebook as @Inbox.

EverNote will set up your first notebook upon signing up. It is called the" [username}'s notebook." It is the location where all of your notes go unless you place them to another location. This default notebook serves as a temporary location for your notes. You should transfer and arrange them in their appropriate notebook as soon as possible. Eventually, you have to name your default notebook as Inbox so that you will always be reminded to check all new notes.

Adding the "@" symbol at the beginning of a notebook name will keep that notebook on top of your notebook list.

2. Creating your table of contents by using Note Links.

A notebook is a compilation of notes. For you to have an easy time sorting your notes, it will be helpful to create your notebook's table of contents.

a. Proceed to the notebook that you like to have a table of contents.
b. Choose, "all notes."
c. Right-click your mouse and select "Copy Note Links."
d. Paste all the content in a new note.
e. Give your note a title.
f. Click the alarm clock on top of the new note for you to set its reminder.

3. Back up blog posts with the IFTTT (If This, Then That)

The IFTTT app automatically feeds blog posts in your account as soon as you publish them. This is done by setting up the IFTTT command "Grab my RSS feed and every time there's a new blog post, make it a note in EverNote."

4. Using checkboxes to assign action items.

Just highlight the action item, then use the checkbox.

5. Feeding to-do app by using the action items of EverNote.

Organize your to-do tasks by checking the boxes. With this, you can easily identify your completed tasks and push through with the incomplete tasks.

Tricks for EverNote search

1. Finding the previous day's notes. Type,

```
created:day-1
```

2. Finding the past 30 days notes with images. Type,

```
resource:image/* created:day-30
```

3. Finding notes with "account" word and encrypted text. Type,

```
account encryption:
```

4. Finding last week's notes with images added with the use of a mobile phone. Type,

```
source:mobile.* created:week-1 resource:image/*
```

5. Finding notes tagged with "tricks" and those which are not labelled with the word "work". Type,

```
tag:tricks -tag:work Evernote
```

6. Finding untagged notes with the title containing "Fwd" and came in through email. Type,

```
intitle:Fwd source:mail.smtp -tag:*
```

7. Finding notes in the notebook Inbox that were created a little more than one month ago. Type,

```
notebook:Inbox -tag:* created:day-30
```

Tags You Should Have

1. to_read – use this for the items that you will read later.

2. to_buy- use for the things you like to buy. You can use this on particular occasions together with the name of the person connected with it.

3. Tags for each member of your family.

4. Tags for every single year from the time you started with EverNote.

5. Tags for every single month

6. Tag your work.

7. Tag with "*frequent". Those tags beginning with a * will appear above your tag list.

8. Tag receipts.

9. Tag inspiration, for some inspirational words and encouragement.

Tags that you should Avoid

1. The term "interesting" and also adjectives such as cool, awesome and other related words.

2. The term "reference".

Notebooks that you should have

1. Wishlist notebook- you can share this with your family and friends to know what you like during your birthday or any special occasion.

2. Individual Projects at home and at work- to have an organized file for your projects.

3. Temp- you can use this to place all the notes that you like to share.

4. Inbox- when set as default, all notes will go here first.

5. Archive- all other notes not assigned to a particular notebook end up here.

Additional Tips

1. Curating your notes.

2. Tagging liberally but intelligently.

3. Choosing a plural or singular convention for tags.

4. Press shift+click on the icon of the elephant,

5. To generate a PDF coming from the page and then add the PDF to the default notebook.

6. Immediately find and delete misspelled tags.

7. Make sure that your EverNote is organized for easy searching.

8. Tagging your notes with the full names of people and in capital letters.

9. As much as possible stay with the simple options and just edits it if necessary.

With all the things discussed, it is proven that EverNote is really a very useful and functional tool not only for students but also for professionals.

IPHONE/IOS HACKS

1. Hacks with Siri

a. You can know the tweets of your friends without even opening the application. You can do this by asking Siri, "What's (Twitter account name) saying?"

b. You can obtain detailed information about available planes and flights by asking Siri, "Planes overhead?"

c. You can play and control Spotify by setting up the account.

d. You can ask direction by using "via transit" to come up with Google maps instead of the Apple maps.

2. Shaking your iPhone from side to side will erase your mistake and you can start typing again.

3. To have a personalized password other than the four digit default pin, proceed to the Settings, choose General, then select Passcode Lock and then choose Turn Off Simple Passcode. You can now enter your new password.

4. If you like to encode numbers without shifting to the number keys, just hold the 123 key and then slide the numbers you will use.

5. You can view your most visited locations by going to the Settings, choosing Privacy, and then Location Services.

6. To adjust the brightness of your phone's screen light, just go to Settings, and then choose General, select Accessibility and choose Turn on Invert Colors.

7. For taking multiple photos quickly, just press and hold your cameras shutter button.

8. To avoid unnecessary downloading or purchasing when others are using your phone, just proceed to Settings, then General, select Accessibility and the choose Turn on Guided Access.

9. To type different website suffixes automatically, just press and hold your phone's full stop key to open up that option.

10. You are able to take pictures with the volume button on your phone and the + volume key on your earphones.

11. You can use a blue tooth keyboard for typing.

12. You can control the video and audio scrubbing by dragging the bar to your desired part.

13. You can see the time stamp on the messages by simply sliding to the left of a conversation.

14. Your keyboard can be switched to thumb mode for a more comfortable typing experience. You can do this by swiping two fingers through the keyboard. You can also choose the "dock and merge" key that is located on the bottom right corner of your keyboard and then drag it up.

15. Putting your phone to airplane mode will enable it to charge two times faster.

16. You can try to use the Google Maps offline when you are travelling abroad. While you still have an internet access, search the location that you need. Enter "ok maps" for it to be cached when you use it offline.

17. Slide from left to the right on the screen of the Calculator app to delete any extra zeroes.

18. You can open your Camera application without unlocking the iPhone. Just swipe on the camera icon that you will find in the bottom right part of your home screen.

19. The Compass application has a level gauge that is built-in. Just open the app and then swipe going to the left to go to the level screen.

20. To easily move on top of the application you are working on, simply tap on the top bar.

21. You can put in more application to the home page and put additional folders for you to be able to access your apps easily.

22. You can tap your space bar two times when you are at the end of a sentence. This will automatically put a period and then a space and the next letter will be capitalized.

23. You can move to the previous or next track with the use of your earphones' remote. Pressing once will play or pause it, pressing twice will move to the next track and pressing three times will let you move to the former track.

24. You can switch between numeric and alpha keyboard by clicking the 123 keys and then sliding up the character and when you release the key, its screen will switch automatically to alpha keyboard.

25. To remove banner notifications, swipe the notification from right to left.

26. For auto-correction, type an extra character when you are spelling a contraction.

27. You can reduce the motion by going to Settings, and then General, choose Accessibility and then Reduce Motion. This makes folder zooms switch to simple cross-fades, thus making it appear that the movement is faster.

28. You can edit your mailboxes by ticking on the mailboxes that you like to see and arrange them according to your preference.

29. You can share your photos with iCloud. You can easily share images and photos to other iCloud accounts.

30. You can hide the apps that are not always being used on a second page of a folder.

31. You can define spelling errors with the auto-correct function. Just proceed to the General, then Keyboard and move to shortcuts. You can now enter most of your misspelled words.

32. You can add several fingerprints on your Touch ID. You can use both your index and thumb fingers.

33. You can connect an external microphone for a better audio quality by using a USB hub with power. This can be done especially when you are conducting interviews or for voice editing.

34. Using your jail broken phone, you can rename Bluetooth devices just by editing one file.

35. You can make visual speed dial icons right on your home screen.

36. You can automatically dial and save phone extensions on your phone.
The hacks, tips and tricks presented are helpful for you iPhone and iPad users. Some of you may not be aware of those hacks. Now you have every chance to maximize the functions of your gadget.

YouTube Hacks

YouTube is one of the most popular and most visited video streaming websites. It always comes first when you want to watch simple tutorials or music videos and movies. There are still some features and tricks of the sites that are not known to many users.

YouTube URL Tricks and Hacks

1. Selecting a specific start time

You can send to anyone a link or an embedded part of a video that you like. You just type "#t=[specific time] at the end of the link. The same way applies to an embedded code, just add the "#t=[specific time] at the end of the embedded code.

2. Skipping unwanted parts

If you want to skip to some unwanted parts and proceed directly to 30% of the clip, just add "&wadsworth=1" on the links' end.

3. Bypassing Regional Restriction

You can bypass the restriction by changing the URL. An example is, https://www.youtube.com/watch?v=F-mjl63e0ms, you have to change it to https://www.youtube.com/v/F-mjl63e0ms

4. Using the auto replay of a video

You can use the looping feature of YouTube. Just use "infinitelooper" instead of "youtube." This will automatically direct you to a third-party platform of YouTube where you can find an option to loop selected parts of the video of your choice.

5. Repeating YouTube playback

You can do this by adding something to the URL. An example is, https://www.youtube.com/watch?v=LQ2t5e7stVM and then change it to https://www.yourepeat.com/watch?v=LQ2t5e7stVM.

6. Using the High-Definition Video Play

You can set the video quality to high-definition or HD format instead of the default lower quality resolution. You can get the extension "Magic Actions for YouTube" on Google Chrome or Firefox. Choose the option to enable Auto HD and choose the resolution you prefer. You can also set the volume.

7. Viewing high quality videos

You can simply add &fm=22" (for 1280x720 resolution, stereo) or "&fmt=18" (for 480x270 resolution,stereo) to URL's end.

8. Embedding Higher Video Quality

To achieve this, you need to add "&ap=%2526fmt%3D22" or "&ap=%2526fmt%3D18" to the URLs end.

9. Looping and Embedded Video

In order to replay embedded videos after they are finished, you have to add "&loop=1" to the links end.

10. Autoplaying Embedded videos

You just need to add "&autoplay=1" to the links end.

11. Disabling Related Videos

If you don't need any videos related to the embedded video you are using, you just need to add"?rel=0" to the links end.

12. Using the Speed Checker

You can check the video's loading speed by adding the term "my_speed" after the address of the home page. If you forgot the URL, you can right click a video and choose "Take speed test."

YouTube Watching Tricks and Hacks

1. Setting the playback quality of the default video

You can do this by going to the "YouTube playback setting" and then click on "Always choose the best quality for my connection and player size" and click on the checkbox "Always play HD on fullscreen (when available)".

2. Preloading entire videos

If you want to preload the entire video to avoid waiting for the video to load, you just have to disable the DASH (Dynamic Adaptive Streaming over HTTP).

3. Watching Videos using a slow internet connection.

You just proceed to http://www.youtube.com/feather_beta. It limits the features to the amount of bytes.

4. Watching YouTube with the Firefox Sidebar

You can watch videos while you are browsing, just install the Firefox Sidebar extension.

5. Automatically Pausing for YouTube video

Install the YouTube Smart Pause, this lets you pause videos when you shift to another tab.

6. Using YouTube Doubler

This app allows you to watch YouTube videos in a slow motion, with 0.25 or 0.5 speed.

YouTube Downloading and Searching Tricks

1. Searching with the Accurate Keyword

Just add "allintitle;" before the title to be able to screen the list that will pop up.

2. Searching by duration/type/upload date/others

You can filter the search results according to the duration, type, upload date and others.

3. Omitting keywords

You can omit some keywords to minimize the links that will appear. Just use, "keyword –excluded keyword."

4. Extracting audio from videos

With YouTube-mp3.org, you can copy and paste the URL to the box and then convert the video. After converting the file, you can download the MP3 to the computer.

Tools for Making your YouTube Browsing and Sharing More Interesting

1. Using TubeReplay

This website will let any YouTube video play again and again. Just type the URL of the video.

2. Using DragonTape

This application lets you remix several YouTube videos. You just have to look for the videos that you like, drag and then drop to the app to arrange the order. You can share the list with your friends with the auto-generated URL or have it embedded with the provided code.

3. Using YouTube Doubler

This can be used in comparing two videos or mashing them together. Just type the URLs of the two videos, choose your VJ name and start with the process. You can easily share the video you did via the auto-generated URL.

4. Using SynchTube

Synchronized videos can be watched with this application. It can be watched with a maximum of 50 other persons, it has a chat window and you can set up a "room" like in chat. You just have to type the URL of all the videos that you like to watch and then you can share the video's URL to the group.

5. Using Infinitube

You can have an infinite list of videos based on the keywords that you will enter.

6. Using Splicd

This application allows you to cut a video by encoding the start time and the end time. You can do this by adding "#t=MMmSSs"(MM stands for minutes, SS stands for seconds) at the end of the link. You can share the edited clip with the use of the auto-generated URL or the provided embed code.

7. Using TubeChop

This is almost similar to Splicd. In addition, it allows you to make an edited portion by swiping a bar along the timeline.

8. Using YouCube

It allows you to create a video cube. You just have to enter six videos that you like to appear on the cubes sides. It will produce a 3d cube that is spinning, you can share it by using a shortened link.

9. Using MixTube

This tool allows you to share and create your own music playlist by adding the links to the list.

10. Using YouFlow

It lets you view your playlist in a layout that has a flow-style. You just need to type in the keywords and the results will automatically be in the layout. You can select to play multiple or single videos.

11. Using Quietube

This will let you watch videos in plain black or plain white background. Just install the app and then click on the button after pressing play.

12. Using YouTube TestTube

This serves as the "ideas incubator" of YouTube. This is where you can look around the comment search, music discovery features, caption editor, HTML5 and others.

13. Using Yahoo's JumpCut

You can use this tool to edit or combine different videos even your own clip or video.

14. Using Gmail's Xoopit

This tool allows you to run and sort through the links of YouTube videos that you have in your inbox. They can also be played right from Gmail.

15. Using the tool "Better YouTube"

This is a Firefox extension that lets you put videos in wide-screen, keeps videos from playing automatically, has a background without distraction, and embeds URL on every video.

16. Using VidToMP3

You can use this tool to record and convert videos to MP3 format.

17. Using TimeTube

This is a video creator of a timeline. This lets you organize news clips and TV shows, view trends and some net-related and current topics. It helps you to narrow down the results list of your searches.

18. Using Miro

Miro Player will turn your desktop into a TiVo for internet video. This software allows you to track the videos you have watched; it automatically recycles other videos and also handles video streams. It can also handle any video format.

19. Using YouTube Podcaster

This is a free tool from the site vixy.net. This makes videos easy to watch and grab. You just need to copy the link in iTunes and enter it to the search box.

20. Watching YouTube on TV

You can add some YouTube capabilities to your X-box or Windows Media Center by using Yougle. With this you can watch the videos right from your classic Xbox.

21. Downloading videos

There are several ways to download videos. Users of Internet Explorer can use the YouTube File Hack. Firefox users can use the "Better YouTube," the All-In-One Video Bookmarklet is a conversion tool that can also be used. You can also use Viddownloader and Vixy.net for downloading video clips. The VLC player can be used for watching FLV format files and videos.

Special Features

1. YouTube Disco
You can have a music playlist of the artist by typing in the artist's name or the song name.

2. YouTube Editor
You can edit your video before uploading it. You can add some effects on your video.

3. YouTube Audio Library
You can download free music with this tool.

4. YouTube Trends
To know the current hottest and most popular videos, you can use this tool.

5. YouTube Movies/TV shows
There is also this tool that you can use to locate TV shows and movies.

6. YouTube Safety Mode
This allows you to filter the inappropriate items on YouTube.

7. YouTube Watch Later Playlist
You can set the time that you want to watch the videos you choose.

YouTube's Amusement

1. Missile Command
A missile game starts when you enter 1980 when playing a video. You will act as a soldier and you need protect the screen from being damaged.

2. Fibonacci
You can see it when you search for the term on YouTube.

3. Use the force, Luke

When you search the "Use the Force, Luke," All of the things in your screen will be shaking left to right and upside down.

4. Beam me up, Scotty

When you enter this title, you will see the effect and animation from Star Trek.

5. Do the Harlem Shake

Typing the "do the harlem shake" will make you do the harlem shake for you.

Other Features

1. Know the YouTube ratings

For you to see both the likes and the dislikes on all videos as well as their ratings, you just need to use the tool Ratings Preview for YouTube. You can use this if you are not sure of the movie that you like to watch, and base your choice from others point of view.

There is really more to it than just watching videos and movie clips. YouTube is really amazing and very useful. You can maximize the entertainment you will get with all its features, tips, tricks and hacks. That is the wonderful world of YouTube.

CONCLUSION

You want to get things organized and in place. You want tasks to be accomplished as soon as possible. You want activities to flow smoothly.

You don't have to worry too much if you encounter some problems. All your problems have solutions. Some may not be easily solved but there sure is a way to fix them. Who would not want to make things better and easier?

In our modern world, some things seem to look very complicated but there are tips, tricks and hacks to help make things easier and better. The technology hacks, tips and tricks included in this e-book gave way to new discoveries. You just have to be practical and creative to know that those simple things mean big and can do great. Some of the hacks are just so simple but you might not be aware of them. Some are also amazing and helpful in boosting the performance of the applications and software you use. You just have to explore and use them to learn and know more about them. You need to apply the things that you've learned to have first-hand experience. You can also prove the strength and effectiveness of the tricks if you apply it to your work. It is a good feeling to know that there are ways to accomplish our tasks faster and easier with the remedies and techniques that are discovered by common people and experts.

The functions of the tools, gadgets, software and applications that we use daily can be improved with the hacks and tricks presented. Don't think twice about following and doing them yourself because they are provided to help you. Be smart and practical. Don't waste time worrying too much.

Life hacks are simple and cunning ways that simplify your life. Almost all of them help you save money by reducing the number of things you need to buy, because what you need is often already at home. They help you save money on groceries and food because you are able to make them last longer. These nifty techniques not only help us save money, but also improve our general quality of life. There is a satisfaction that we can get when we see how clever we have been and how we have utilized and used everything. We are able to work better, be more effective and efficient, and more productive when we have everything organized.

Want to read more exciting stories for FREE?

Join my **V.I.P** List now!

I regularly GIVEAWAY FREE books and SPECIAL DISCOUNTS!

Join my mailing list and be one of thousands we already receiving FREEBIES!

Join by visiting this site:

http://www.ravenspress.com/freeselfhelp/

Or Scan this QR Code from your smartphone to go the website directly

Printed in Germany
by Amazon Distribution
GmbH, Leipzig